MEXICAN MURAL

MEXICAN MURAL

THE STORY OF MEXICO, PAST AND PRESENT

LOIS HOBART

ILLUSTRATED
WITH PHOTOGRAPHS

HARCOURT, BRACE & WORLD, INC., NEW YORK

TO MY SON TONY
AND HIS NEW GENERATION OF
HEMISPHERIC AMERICANS

Foreword

No country can be bound within a book, certainly not one as complex as Mexico. And no one can undertake the writing of a book like this without a sense of humility and responsibility. Nor can one person hope to present, even fleetingly, all facets to the entire satisfaction of people who live in the country, study it, or visit it.

Reactions to Mexico are extremely varied and seldom lukewarm. A visitor becomes an ardent lover of the country or detests it heartily, and Mexico has so many different aspects and personalities that each visitor sees it with different eyes. There is the cosmopolitan Mexico of the capital, the whirling traffic of large cities, the primitive Mexico of the anthropologists and archeologists, the tourist landmarks and the colonial cities and quiet villages, the vast deserts and the sky-scraping mountains.

In both text and illustrations I have tried for a realistic mixture, a representation of both the color and the grime of Mexico, the splendors and the shortcomings—a balanced survey intended to offer readers:

1. Some concrete information about Mexico.
2. A feeling for the differences between the Mexican temperament and way of life and that which prevails in the United States of America.

5

3.   A minimum of background for understanding the
      relationship between the two countries and their
      people.

4.   A comprehension of the fact that in Mexico his-
      torical and geographic forces have molded per-
      haps the most *American* of any people in the
      Western Hemisphere, a blending of Indian blood
      with Spanish (and that of other European peo-
      ples), Moorish, Jewish, as well as some Oriental
      and Negro that has become specifically and dis-
      tinctively Mexican.

5.   An idea of the future of Mexico as one of the
      great countries of the world in its vigor, culture,
      accomplishments, and potentialities.

To the reader without any background knowledge of
Mexico, it should be pointed out that variations in the
spelling of names (for example, Montezuma and Moctezuma, Cortés and Cortéz) occur partly because of the
difficulty of representing Indian names in Spanish spelling
and partly because the Spaniards themselves used variations
of their own names.

I should like to express here my deep appreciation of
the help and cooperation of a number of people who have
taken an interest in this book. Jovita Zubaran of the Biblioteca Benjamin Franklin in Mexico City has not only bom-
barded me with books, charts, and information but has also
been a patient and critically attentive reader of the manuscript. Sr. Robert Parker and Sr. Guillermo Aldana of the
Tourist Bureau have provided me with a large share of the
photographs used and have read the manuscript besides.
Mary Parsons of the library of Mexico City College has

also sent books. Long-term residents like Mr. and Mrs. Ted French have offered material and suggestions. Stirling Dickinson, Director of the Instituto Allende of San Miguel de Allende, has given me material, read the manuscript, and offered suggestions. Sr. Esteban Garaiz of the Academia Hispano-Americana of San Miguel has given the manuscript a last-minute reading. And my husband, Harold Black, has aided me immeasurably in encouragement, interest, and the maintenance of balance in this brief survey of Mexico.

Unfortunately, I cannot list all the people to whom I have talked and from whom I have received information, but my gratitude extends no less to them for being un-named. Let me hope that the book will reflect their help in authenticity, interest, and usefulness.

Lois Hobart

San Miguel de Allende
Gto., México
March, 1963

Preface

Volumes have been written about Mexico past and present; yet this small book, describing in clear and concise language many as yet untouched aspects of Mexican life, constitutes an excellent survey of human activity south of the border.

The author has done well to include an historical background, which is necessary for the correct interpretation of present-day Mexico. Here is a country in which the past runs into the present and is kept alive in every conceivable way with fervid nationalism. It is the favorite theme for artists and writers, and modern architecture takes its place alongside pre-Hispanic pyramids, colonial churches, and other vestiges of long ago. Burros and Indians jog along the roads with automobiles whizzing past, and radios play the latest hits in the most humble adobe huts.

The people are innate lovers of art in all its manifestations and are especially sensitive to color and music. When they are gay, they are very gay, and when they are sad, they are also very, very sad. This is especially true of the mestizo. The fusion of the Indians with the Spanish conquerors, which began a century before the Pilgrims landed in Plymouth, was the first and foremost step in the forma-

9

tion of the mestizo, the true Mexican, who thereby inherits a Latin temperament tinged with Indian stoicism and melancholy. True, not all Mexicans are dark: there are many blue-eyed blonds and even redheads, but these are in the minority.

With accurate and realistic descriptions, Lois Hobart portrays life in a variety of conditions, omitting nothing that might make the picture more complete. A keen observer and a meticulous writer, she has made this book a true guide to Mexico.

Jovita T. Zubaran
Anthropologist and Assistant Librarian of the
Biblioteca Benjamin Franklin,
Mexico, D.F., Mexico
September, 1962

Contents

Contents

MEXICAN MURAL

1

"There Are No Fixed Rules"

On his first visit to Mexico, Charles Flandrau, a young writer, glanced out of the window at a torrent of rain and asked his Mexican hostess whether it rained as much in summer as in winter. The lady regarded him thoughtfully and spoke at last a pearl of wisdom: *"No hay reglas fijas, señor."* In Mexico, it is true, there are no fixed rules.

There can be no better introduction to Mexico than those words. Everything has its exceptions. Facts are hard to come by, statistics often a joke. It is notably a country where anything can happen. Life is unpredictable, at one moment sunny and tranquil and at the next cataclysmic. Life does not conform to our North American notions of order, reason, logic, and common sense. It is not a sensible country to our way of thinking. But it is thoroughly *sensible* in the Spanish sense—sensitive, perceptive, alive.

Mexico is an incorrigibly romantic country of magical charm and paradox. "Everyone's experience is different," Flandrau wrote in his charming book, *Viva Mexico!*, "and everyone, in a sense, is a pioneer groping his way —like Cortés on his prodigious march up from the sea. One never knows, from the largest to the smallest cir-

cumstances of life, just what to expect, and Ultimate
Truth abideth not."

What is the *real* Mexico? It is a mosaic of many elements. You find it in the tireless trot of burros under
mountains of sugar cane or alfalfa or dried corn. You
find it in the bus that trundles out of nowhere, picks
up passengers on a nearly deserted road, and lurches
through a valley or up a mountainside; in taxis that
whirl through the cities and ancient vehicles that grum-
ble noisily over the cobble-stoned streets of villages.
You hear it in the shuffle of the feather dancers, in the
clicking of heels in the hat dance, in the rhythmic slap
of hands patting out tortillas, or the clop of horses' hoofs
in the street. At night you hear it in the serenade of
mariachis, strolling musicians, under a balcony in Jalisco.
You smell it in the fragrance of fresh pineapple or
roasted corn in the market, in the *tacos* sizzling in oil.

You feel the hunger of Mexico with the beggars in
the streets and the starving yellow-eyed dogs underfoot
at the butcher's stall. You sense its harshness in the dust
and aridity of winter months, in the crazy winds of February and March, in the torrential downpours of summer
that carve deeper gullies into the naked earth.

Mexico is the pilgrimage of 100,000 worshipers walking a hundred miles to a shrine. It is the labor of an
Indian woman hacking with machete for firewood with
her baby cradled behind her in a *rebozo*, a long stole.
It is also the elegance of a dinner by candlelight at
Delmonico's; the dash of *charros* (gentlemen riders) into
an arena; the shout of *Olé!* at a bullfight and the hush as a
matador sights for the kill. It's the childish refrain, *Alo,
cinco* (Hello, five centavos), and a smile from an outra-

geously dirty face. It's the stenographer in the bank, the *campesino* (countryman) plodding to market, the young businessman catching a plane, the domino players at a sidewalk café. It's the everlasting *Aqui no hay, Quién sabe?, Mañana,* and *Momentito* (We don't have it here, Who knows?, Tomorrow, and A tiny moment). It is the conviction that time is no commodity to be chopped into chunks of minutes and hours but a dimension of life not to be measured by clocks.

And Mexicans are as varied as their country. There are stoic, broad-cheeked Indian faces with solemn remembering dark eyes. There are narrow Spanish heads with heritage of Moorish, Jewish, and Iberian-Roman blood; the Nordic foreigner's fair skin and blue eyes; the full-lipped Negroes, descendants of escaped slaves mixed with Indians; and most common of all, the mestizo, the mixture of Indian and Spaniard.

The Mexican bears the trace of all of these. By turns he is violent and patient, affectionate and cruel, stubborn and pliant, shrewd and slow. He is hardworking and lazy in the sun, religious and fiercely antichurch. He is indifferent to time, death, and schedules. Yet he is attentive to seasons, fiestas, the needs of the earth, the stomach, the soul, the pleasures of the senses in color, form, texture, and sound. Unless you understand something of the Mexican temperament, you will never understand Mexico.

Forget for the moment cities like your own and look with fresh eyes at a Mexican village. At first all villages look alike. But as you see more of the country, you detect subtle variations. Sit first in the plaza, which is the heart of the village, because here is Mexico in miniature.

The bench of cement or iron you sit on is marked with the name of its donor. Overhead, green palm or banana trees droop their sworded leaves or Indian laurels form tall boxed hedges where the branches begin ten or fifteen feet above the ground. Here and there a jacaranda sprays its lavender-blue spring blossoms or a pine tree towers above the others. Plots of grass are crisscrossed by walks radiating from a bandstand, bordered with roses, calla lilies, cannas, or geraniums.

Across from the plaza stands the municipal palace with imposing, thick stone walls and colonial arches, as much fortress as administrative office. In it are the offices of the mayor and his staff, and perhaps representatives of Hacienda, the federal government. On another side of the plaza may be the *parroquia* (the main church), baroque and elaborate, rosy stone or green, depending on local quarries. It is magnificent outside and lavish with gold and silver within. On either side of the plaza are arcades fronting principal hotels, stores, and restaurants.

Adjoining or near the plaza is the market. This is usually a large building surrounded by scores of white-tented umbrellas, booths, and stands where food, flowers, clothing, footwear, pottery, and baskets are sold. Here the people meet to shop, sell, flirt, and gossip. There are tiny dim restaurants with hard benches and tables. Women stir bubbling caldrons of soup or frijoles (beans) or fry tacos (tortillas stuffed with meat, fowl, or cheese, and fried). Others have baskets of fresh tortillas miraculously kept warm in towels. Men tend little glass-enclosed stands with an electric light bulb to warm mounds of *carnitas* (cooked meat, usually pork). Worshipers kneel at a small shrine inside the market. Dogs, children, and babies wander around, the smallest babies kept in boxes or the mother's rebozo.

From the plaza you gaze down streets of walled adobe or stone houses. The finest are two stories or higher, with pretty balconies adorned with iron grillwork and with massive doors of green or brown weathered wood decorated with enormous locks, bolts, and metalwork. First-floor windows are guarded with iron bars and carved wooden shutters. To us, accustomed to lawns around modern frame or brick houses, the effect of these blank walls is at first bleak and forbidding. Later we admire the privacy and grace of the patios behind the walls.

Most walls are of crumbling or patched adobe. A few are freshly painted. Others bear rainbow patches of pastels from previous coats of pale yellow, blue, rose, or green paint. Through an open doorway or wrought-iron gate you glimpse a patio—with a tiled fountain, colonial archways, walls green with morning glory vines or the vines of purple, orange and scarlet bougainvillea. In the evening there is a waft of strong perfume from night-blooming jasmine or the datura with its white trumpet-shaped flowers.

Nearby is the entrance of a poorer house with a patio of dirt. Even here there are the flowerpots of geraniums, an avocado, orange, or lime tree, towering poinsettias, and walls covered with flowering vines. On the edge of town are little suburbs of adobe huts, each with a tiny plot of land bordered with organ cactus.

The plaza has hardly changed in three or four hundred years. Only now over the narrow cobbled streets bicy-

cles whiz past; buses, taxis, and cars nudge burros, add-
ing noise, carbon monoxide, and the hustle of the twen-
tieth century. Red Pepsi-Cola and Coca-Cola signs flaunt
overhead. In store windows American products are guar-
anteed to stop any but the wealthy from purchase—$1
for a 20-cent can of chocolate syrup, $400 for a refrig-
erator of modest size, $4,000 or more for a car that sells
for $2,300 in the United States.

Who are the actors on this stage? Black-eyed shoe-
shine boys with kits of brushes, rags, and polish. A public scribe taking dictation from an illiterate campesino
whose daughter lives far away. Taxi drivers chatting or
reading newspapers near vehicles new and ancient. Children playing, attended by maids, nurses, mothers, or
older brothers and sisters.

And the vendors. A man carries on his head an immense basket of bread and rolls. Another bears a bouquet
of balloons—red, green, purple, blue, and yellow. A
little girl offers artificial carnations and lilies—a quaint
touch in this land of flourishing tropical flowers. A candy
merchant wields a seven-foot stick of scarlet sweets. One
lad totes a tall stack of birdcages with bright-feathered
parrots, parakeets, and canaries for sale. A countryman
strides by with two bleating kids slung over his shoulders
on the way to market. Best of all there is the equivalent
of our Good Humor man with his shabby cart, singing
out *"Pa-le-e-e-tas"* to advertise his wares of fruit-flavored
ices.

A charro rides by and reins in to speak with a friend.
While he coils his stiff reata, you admire the embossed
saddle, the silver-trimmed bit and spurs, the rakish sombrero. Two *vaqueros* (cowboys) trot past on smaller,

scrubbier mounts. Townspeople saunter in the plaza, read, or sip coffee, hot chocolate or a coke at a sidewalk café. Policemen in khaki stand talking on a corner. A beggar sidles up to ask a few centavos *por caridad* (for charity). You drop a twenty-centavo piece into her palm. She murmurs a blessing and moves away.

Down the street two or three toddlers clad in white undershirts, or nothing at all, play in puddles from yesterday's rain. Church bells begin tolling. Burros trot past laden with wood or pottery. In the distance sound the lively and rasping strains of a school band—and you soon relax into an Indian world of timelessness and forget the pressures of business or errands.

People pass in and out of the church. Women wear dark rebozos; little girls cover their heads with gayer miniature shawls. Men enter with sombreros in hand. The priest emerges with a coat thrown over his vestments.

Costumes, like customs, have altered in recent years. Some countrymen still wear the pajamalike white shirt and trousers, but most dress in blue jeans, shirt, and jacket. On cool mornings they swathe themselves to the ears in a scrape or wear the sleeveless wool jacket called a *chaleco*. Women wear factory-made clothes more and more but retain the rebozo—sometimes worn under the sombrero in a style reminiscent of the Peruvian Indians, especially in the fields or on pilgrimages. This useful article, introduced by the Spanish, is indispensable as a cradle for the baby, protection from the weather, carryall for food, bedding at night. Young girls wear it in a variety of ways for decoration. The *quexquemetl* of pre-Conquest days—two pieces of cotton or

woolen cloth sewn together—survives as a triangular
shoulder covering. So does the *jorongo*, the cloak of
two long straight pieces of cloth with a neck opening.
The farther south you go, the more you see of older
costumes, some of them markedly Oriental.

Even in this serene village the pace changes as time
passes. A respectable first-class bus arrives to deposit
its passengers and luggage, and urchins cluster around
clamoring to be hired as porters or guides. Then a sec-
ond-class bus rumbles by laden with passengers, crates
of freight, birdcages, bunches of poultry, tires, chairs,
a couple of pigs, a lamb or two. The bus struggles uphill
and stops, and passengers descend to help push it over
the crest of the hill. At noon the children burst out of
the schools and throng down to the center of town to
buy notebooks, pencils, pens, and sweets, meet their
cronies, play jukebox and pinball machines, and finally
stroll home for lunch and homework until the afternoon
session begins about three o'clock.

This is typical of a Mexican village of the central
plateau or the north. In a fishing village or a southern
town where northern industry has penetrated less, the
tempo and pattern are somewhat different. There are
fewer cars, more homemade carts, less traffic. The people more often wear the traditional costumes. The landscape differs too, with jungle or swampland or ocean
beaches. The weather is warmer and more humid, and
mosquito netting and hammocks come into play.

Fiesta! No glimpse of Mexican life is complete without
a fiesta. In the United States we celebrate one holiday
a year with fireworks. The Mexicans have dozens. Every

few weeks there is fresh cause for celebration, and fireworks are indispensable. There are important religious holidays, like days of patron saints, the Day of the Three Kings on January 6, Shrove Tuesday (*Carnaval*), Easter, the Day of the Dead with its nightlong vigil for the departed, and the posadas that precede Christmas and represent the search of Mary and Joseph for a lodging. There are the national holidays to honor independence, Constitution Day, or the victory over the French at Puebla on May 5, 1862. There are local fiestas for a town or neighborhood to plead for rain.

Tonight there is a small neighborhood fiesta of the Santa Cruz at the church of that name. It occurs not on May 3, its proper day, but on the weekend of the sixth and seventh so that the country people who come to market on Sunday can join in the fun.

For three days the streets leading to the church have been bright with fluttering strips of colored tissue paper wired diagonally across from house to house. At eight o'clock a brass band sounds lustily from afar, and the crowd gathers. Along the street tables and booths have been set up under naked light bulbs. Tacos, enchiladas, and other delicacies are temptingly displayed. Tubs of ice are being shaved into little red and green clay jugs, to which are added colored water and juices for the thirsty. Vendors lug wide baskets of cracklings, the crisp skin of roast pig, to set up on portable stools. Small boys cry out their wares of popcorn—*palomitas* (little doves).

The band assembles in the churchyard beside the hill above the recently finished swimming pool and the municipal waterworks. By day the bandsmen are carpenters, tailors, masons, and barbers. By night they don uniforms of dark blue with gold trim and kepis—at least some of them do. But some, less mindful of glamor, come in ordinary shirts and trousers or even T-shirts. There are some excellent city bands and orchestras, like the symphonic band of Oaxaca, for instance, but in smaller towns the bands aim for loudness rather than musical merit. Their audience loves music in all forms and approves all attempts to perform.

With few pleasures, Mexicans know how to extract the utmost delight from all entertainment and understand well the value of anticipation. They are willing to wait hours for the main feature of the evening. When you ask at what time the fireworks are scheduled, someone answers agreeably but erroneously, "In half an hour." Inevitably it is three hours later that the first fireworks begin. Meanwhile, you enjoy the vignettes around you.

Little boys stroll arm in arm. Parents climb the steps with sleeping babies draped limply on their shoulders or tucked into a rebozo with one little fist dangling. Girls in full-skirted print dresses and petticoats and high-heeled slippers step in and out of church with lace mantillas over their heads. A little boy teases, laughs, and embraces his doting, gray-haired grandmother. Three girls while away the time by spinning flat round discs along a bench.

Many girls wear their hair in loose waves or hanging below their waists. Some twine bright ribbons and bows into their long braids and tie them together at the nape of the neck. Others wear their hair short, with permanent waves and the most fashionable of hairdos. Poorer girls wear odd combinations of print and striped blouses and skirts, but occasionally one appears in a cheap but charming frock of simple lines that shows her tiny waist and graceful figure. Older women dress mainly in black (there is usually a death to mourn), but the young people have no scruples about color. Boys and men cheerfully combine a magenta or orange shirt with blue market-bought trousers. Girls put together colors with effects sometimes garish but often striking or subtle.

Small children are decked in fancy hand-embroidered clothes for special occasions, ridiculously costly considering the parents' income. Clothes of the poorer children rarely fit, and a tawdry satin or chiffon dress hangs pitifully to the ankles of a little girl, while her brother's patched shirt is much too large or too small.

A young campesino squats on his heels beside a grave, fine-featured Indian girl and exclaims, *"Qué milagro!"* (A chance meeting is always a miracle.) The girl smiles at him shyly over her gray rebozo and makes room for him among her companions.

At last rockets begin to snake yellow trails into the dark sky, curving out with white sparks and plunging to the earth in showers of blue and pink. Children scramble to snatch the still-glowing crowns when they land. A *globo* (or a star or cube instead of a globe) of white, blue, and green tissue paper bearing candles inside rises into the air and floats above the ninety-foot trees of the park below. Other fireworks burst into frenzied circles and spirals on the ground. As usual one misfires, lands on a woman nearby, and burns the rebozo from her back. Casualties are common, sometimes serious, but that adds to the drama and excitement of the occasion.

Then come the *castillos* (castles) that are the climax
of the evening. These are light bamboo frameworks of
castles three or four stories high, rigged with a series
of fireworks that pop off in elaborate sequences for a
half hour at a time with hisses, blasts, and shrieks. Finally
a man appears on the roof of the church, silhouetted
against the strings of light bulbs slanting from tower
to ground. With a long wand he sets off still more fireworks on the strings and lights the cross that burns in
a fiery climax. Everyone comes to the fiesta—Indian,
mestizo, countryman, townsman, aristocrat, foreigner, and
tourist.

The mestizos and the Indians live much of their lives
in the streets, enjoying them, using them as parlor, kitchen, nursery, dining room, bedroom (and bathroom),
as Anglo-Saxons have not done since the Middle Ages.
Children play in the streets till late. They bounce a ball
against a door, play a game something like Going to
New Orleans, or bull and matador, while their parents
sit on the steps with babies in their arms, chatting with
neighbors under a streetlight.

In these scenes one senses deep affection and close
ties between brothers and sisters, so quick to take responsibility for younger children, between children and
parents, among girls, and between men friends who meet
on the street and throw their arms about each other's
shoulders in the *abrazo* (embrace).

What one may not so easily sense is that the warmth
and affection do not preclude violence and catastrophe.
The pervasive ghosts of Indian forebears—religious, tribal, and secular—linger still. At any time the earthquake
rumbling beneath the tranquil village life might erupt

in tragedy—in a drunken quarrel about a girl, the knifing of an enemy, a riot against some new law, the shooting of an escaping prisoner—just as the fireworks shot into the crowd in the midst of festivity and burned the rebozo from the woman's back.

There is throughout Mexican life that thread of paradox.

2

Pyramid and Mountain

The very landscape of Mexico is dramatic, befitting a country that has been for centuries a vast theater of extraordinary events. Dust and desert, sun, cactus, and rugged mountains, volcanoes, and jungle, fields of alfalfa and corn, tall stands of pine, rows of gray-green maguey, rusty-colored gorges in the earth, muddy rivers that dry into puddles in winter and rage over their banks in summer, terraced mountains—this is the face of Mexico.

Mexicans call their country—Los Estados Unidos Mexicanos—simply "the Republic." The name of Mexico refers strictly to the capital city and Federal District, which correspond to Washington and the District of Columbia. For convenience we shall follow our own more familiar custom in referring to Mexico and Mexico City. It should be noted too that to a Mexican the name American means any inhabitant of the Americas, and that we ourselves are known as *norteamericanos*.

Mexico has much the shape of a cornucopia, a horn of plenty. It tapers from the 1,800-mile border along the Rio Grande (the Río Bravo del Norte to a Mexican) south to a narrow isthmus of only 124 miles across, then flares northward and east into Yucatán. To the west of the mainland is Baja California, a long slim finger of mountainous land that extends into the Pacific Ocean.

The plenty is there in the earth—silver, gold, tin, copper, lead, zinc, opals, and petroleum, to mention a few of its products—but these lavish mineral resources are hard to exploit because of the rugged terrain. It is peaked with mountains and grooved with canyons that make communication and transportation costly and difficult. The land, once heavily forested and now treeless over large areas, has succumbed to the primitive farming methods of past centuries, to heavy seasonal rainfalls, and to erosion. There are about 6,000 miles of seacoast and many islands along the coasts on both the Atlantic and the Pacific shores.

Deserts, sprawling into Texas, Arizona, and New Mexico, are near wastelands marked by nopal, maguey and organ cactus, mesquite, and faraway mountains. The coasts are lined with hot, humid jungles, where in some regions to the south the rainfall may amount annually to as much as ten feet! Two vast mountain ranges form a deep V into the south and make a great central plateau, between five and eight thousand feet above sea level. This is the most fertile and populous area of the country. On the plateau, ringed and sprinkled with mountains, the rainy season usually comes between May and September or October, and the climate is agreeably warm and not extreme. This is the temperate land. The mountaintops are the cold lands, one degree cooler for every 300 feet of altitude, and the seacoasts and deserts are the hot lands.

Everywhere there are mountains. The country is tormented by earthquakes, volcanoes, hurricanes, and the caprices of rain, especially in the south. Orizaba, highest of the snow-topped peaks, towers over 18,000 feet, and Popocatépetl and its companion Iztaccíhuatl, the White Woman, visible from the capital, are both over 17,000 feet. The youngest volcano, Paricutín, burst into being in 1943 when a farmer tilling his soil looked back to see smoke curling upward from a rising mound of earth. Now it has smothered a nearby town except for one weirdly protruding church steeple, and though quiet since 1952, it still smolders and fumes 9,000 feet above sea level.

Mexico covers 760,373 square miles, but until the nineteenth century, when it lost California, Texas, and the Southwest to the United States, it was the fourth-largest country in the world. Now it is the smallest country of North America but larger than any of its neighbors of Central America and most countries of South America. The Pan-American Highway, which runs through it into Guatemala, symbolizes Mexico's importance as the connecting link between its northern neighbors and the rest of Latin America.

Nomads from Asia are believed to have crossed the frozen Bering Straits on foot at the end of the last glacial age, perhaps 20,000 to 30,000 years ago. They traveled slowly in small groups, living on fish, game, and such nuts, fruits, and vegetables as could be gathered as they moved. They traveled to new sites as the food supply gave out and eventually occupied pockets of land throughout the Western Hemisphere. After generations of isolation and inbreeding, small groups formed into distinct physical types, with a great diversity of language and culture.

These people domesticated only the dog and fowl. Primitive Indians of North America were content to hunt the caribou and bison instead of breeding and domesticating them. In Central America these animals were unknown, at least by the time a real civilization had evolved, as were sheep, horses, donkeys, and goats. In South America the llama and alpaca were beasts of burden and a source of wool. Some American tribes learned the principle of the wheel, but for want of beasts of burden, the wheel was used only for toys.

Eventually the development of agriculture freed these tribes from dependence on hunting. Corn was to the Americas what rice was to Asia and wheat to European nations. It was the heart of the economy, of religion, and of civilization. Beans were another staple, and other plants known to the Indians were squash, sweet potatoes, tobacco, cotton, and herbs. These were largely new to the Europeans, and the transfer of some of them to Europe made it possible for that continent to double its food supply. The Indians also discovered the uses of maguey (of infinite variety, from the supply of pulque, mezcal, and tequila to needles, material for sewing, poultices, thatching for roofs, etc.), henequen, and cochineal, as well as techniques of cultivation.

Agriculture favored the growth of population. It made possible more stable social patterns and regulations, large communities and public projects like irrigation systems, ceremonial centers, the storage of food. This, in turn, permitted the development of a leisure class and of rites and prayers that led to a caste of priests. Unfortunately, the valuable crop of corn or maize was one that quickly exhausted the soil. When a community grew too large, some of its members separated or all moved to a new site with a better food supply. Overpopulation in those days was no problem.

It was more difficult to maintain villages in forest country, where the ground had to be cleared, the soil quickly became depleted, and communities either had to use crop rotation or move to a new site. In open country, where minerals near the surface of the soil could replenish it, permanent villages became possible. There was a chance not only to store equipment and food but to exchange techniques and knowledge and gain more rapidly in tribal experience. There was more leisure then for people to observe and speculate on the change of seasons, the relationship of sun, stars and moon to earthly life, the mysteries of nature.

In Central America and Mexico, the earliest cultures of which we have much knowledge began at the stage where the civilization of the Pueblo Indians of the southwestern United States stopped. The people knew how to cultivate corn, beans, and cotton. They wove cotton for clothing, made pottery for the storage and serving of food, fashioned tools and ornaments of stone, bone and wood. They had a tribal government and a religion centered around the natural forces that control agriculture. They made small sculptures, "village art," showing people at work and play.

Prehistoric civilization contains many mysteries that are gradually being solved by archeologists, anthropologists, and other scientists. Aside from the study of artifacts and remains, one of the most valuable tools of research is the carbon 14 test. This dates with some degree of accuracy (i.e., within a couple of hundred years instead of a thousand years) certain animal bones, textiles, wooden furniture, shells, and charcoal that are recovered from the earth. Living plants and animals discharge radioactive carbon, which disintegrates at the rate of 16 ticks per minute per gram of carbon, a sound that is registered by the Geiger counter. After death, the ticks slow down at a known rate.

The ruins of Zacatenco, Tlatilco, and the more advanced Monte Albán near Oaxaca can be dated by this method as far back as about 1500 B.C. The trend is now toward pushing back the accepted date of early cultures much farther than once seemed possible.

So numerous are the archeological treasures of Mexico that the government can afford to excavate and study only a few major sites. All over the country are spots that elsewhere would excite any amateur or professional digger—small primitive pyramids, burial places and chambers, hidden villages with exposed walls, bits of pottery and figures upturned by plows or a casual foot or brought up by the bucketful in steam shovels. Uxmal, Mitla, Tula, Teotihuacán, Palenque, and Bonampak are only a few of the sites that demand more exploration. The scientific world still awaits the unraveling of the hieroglyphs that will offer further clues.

From 200, 300, and 500 to about 900 A.D., at the time of the Dark Ages in Europe when barbaric hordes overran Italy and the Moors conquered Spain, such American tribes as the Zapotec, the Maya, and the people of Veracruz, Cholula, and the Valley of Mexico experienced their most highly developed, or "classic," periods. Still later came the Aztec and Texcocan tribes.

Try to imagine the awe of two travelers in the nineteenth century when they hacked their way through the green jungle of Honduras to a river and found themselves confronted suddenly with an ancient stone wall towering 100 feet above the brush. The red-bearded New York lawyer, John Lloyd Stephens, and his English artist companion, Frederick Catherwood, brought back the first modern reports of buried cities and marvels of sculpture and work in jade, obsidian, and turquoise from Central America and Yucatán. Even today when the forewarned tourists visit Chichén Itzá, or plunge by jeep through jungle roads and come upon the ruins of Palenque in the sunset, the sight is startling and imposing.

In the winter of 1931-32, when the archeologist Alfonso Caso was beginning the important excavations at Monte Albán above the city of Oaxaca, the workmen dug down through some ruins. Late on a January afternoon they lifted a slab roofing Tomb Seven. An assistant wriggled down into it and found himself up to the ankles in jewelry and precious metals. It was a discovery as sensational as that of the tomb of King Tutankhamen in Egypt in the previous decade.

Inside the tomb were the skeletons of nine men. These ranged in age from a boy of sixteen to the central figure, a man in his sixties, dead of a brain tumor. Around them on the inlaid floor were mosaics of turquoise, gold bells and pearls, and pieces of finely wrought jewelry. There was a human skull inlaid with turquoise, a marvelous cup of rock crystal, pendants, necklaces, belt buckles, earplugs, rings with eagle heads, even jet and amber, as well as jade. The priceless find was jaguar bones carved with Mixtec glyphs, which Caso is still studying with the help of an old Mixtec map. Such finds hold clues to the ancient Zapotec civilizations.

Dr. Manuel Gamio was another of the archeological adventurers. He uncovered preclassic towns going back to 1450 B.C. It was his cook who grew rapturous over the find of a metate, a stone on which corn is ground, several thousand years old but better than any she had seen in the market.

The death in 1957 of Miguel Covarrubias, artist, writer, teacher, and anthropologist, robbed Mexico of one of its outstanding figures. It was he who proposed the theory that the Olmec people of the sculptured smiling features were the ancestors of the other Mexican cultures —and today it is believed that he was correct.

What have we learned about these people of a thousand and two thousand years ago? Much more than can be suggested here, of course. We know they were people of great achievements and artistry, particularly the Maya, whose culture represented the zenith of civilization in the Western Hemisphere at that time. After long study of the stars they perfected a calendar better than any developed in the Old World until centuries later. They used observatories and planned their buildings in accordance with astronomical knowledge. They were the first in history to use numbers involving the concept of zero—an outstanding achievement in science—and they used dots, bars, and placement to form compound numbers.

Those of the American Indians (also called Amerindians) who lived in Mexico were advanced in medicine and had a profound knowledge of herbs and their effects. They studied plants, minerals, soil, and animal and human bodies. They could set fractured bones, knew some surgery, could fill teeth, practiced blood letting, and knew anesthesia and used it on victims for sacrifice. Sweat baths were popular and are still widely used in the provinces. But much medical knowledge of the Indians, often considered merely curious lore by the Spaniards, was lost after the Conquest, and no written record of it remains, though the Indians continued to practice medicine. Many *curanderos* and witch doctors of today use herbs and practices that go back many centuries.

However, in the sixteenth century, Francisco Hernandes, a Spanish doctor, was sent by Philip II to list all the plants used by Mexicans. He expected to complete his work in a few months. Instead he stayed two years, filled eleven notebooks with drawings and thirteen more with text, which were published in three volumes, *The History of the Plants of New Spain*. It covered 1,200 plants, 200 birds and animals, several minerals and types of soil.

In architecture and art Indian accomplishments were spectacular, both in scale and in beauty, though their tools were primitive. Temples were built on pyramids level at the top for sacrifices and rites. Some pyramids were larger than many of those in Egypt. The Indians built palaces, monasteries, ball courts, observatories, canals, and roads. They were artists of space and provided long vistas for their temples, with plazas, terraces, and sculptured monuments to add imposing dignity. Their sculptured murals reflect religious beliefs and much of their daily life. There are such scenes as a chief with his courtiers, offerings to the gods, the disposal of captured warriors.

The Indian calendar allowed for a solar year of 365 days, broken into 18 months of 20 days each, plus 5 days that were considered unlucky. There was also a ritual calendar of 260 days. Every 52 years, the ritual calendar ended on the same day as the solar calendar, and it was believed that the fate of the world was at stake. During the 5 "unlucky" days that preceded the crucial date, people let their fires go out, destroyed household goods, kept their children awake, and extinguished the altar fire that had burned for 52 years. They waited in suspense until the appearance of a certain star in the center of the heavens assured them of the continuity of life. Then priests kindled a new fire and sent runners with torches to light altars in every temple and village. The people cleaned and whitewashed their houses, rebuilt their furnishings, renovated the temples, feasted on special foods, and made sacrifices, rejoicing for the new life awaiting them. Then followed 13 days of dancing, singing, and celebration.

Each day of the ritual calendar bore a different composite name, formed of the name of the day and of an element or animal—lizard, deer, wind, coyote. This was the name given a child born on that day. There was a special class of mathematicians who cast horoscopes.

The Indian cities were separate entities like the city states of Greece or Italy, but they shared many aspects of their culture—the worship of certain gods under different names (e.g., Quetzalcoatl, the feathered serpent of the Aztecs, is known in Maya mythology as Kukulcán), the knowledge of astronomy, customs in raising children, and so on. Often they warred among themselves, mainly to seize victims for sacrifice.

Scientists are still perplexed about the cause of the ebb and flow of Maya civilizations. At various periods these achieved splendid cities and ceremonial centers and then faded away. The most likely cause seems to be not invasion, although traces remain of other strong influences in later cities, but rather a depletion of natural resources around those cities, which led to their abandonment.

Besides the uncertainties about the time and development of these cultures, there is another important riddle to solve. Did these American civilizations attain their heights in isolation, unaided by contacts with Europe or the Orient? Or were there contacts that promoted the spread of new concepts and skills in Middle and South America? In short, were the Indian cultures self-made or did they receive foreign aid?

There are all manner of mysterious likenesses of language, culture, and art between certain areas in the Americas and in Asia. Many Mexicans have a strong Mongoloid cast of feature. Is that a throwback to ancestors who crossed the Bering Straits 20,000 or 30,000 years ago, or have there been more recent contacts? What of the key design of Mitla, so similar in feeling to Greek motifs? What of the Maya figures in the murals so close in feeling and posture to Indo-Chinese murals?

What of the grotesque dancing figures in bas relief at Monte Albán that represent so distinctively Greek, Assyrian, African, and Hindu features? What of the words in some Indian dialects that suggest an Oriental origin?

Some anthropologists explain these mysteries as mere coincidence. Others, known as diffusionists, believe there were transoceanic contacts that diffused some of these concepts and influences. Gordon Willey, an American archeologist, admitted in 1960 that various discoveries had thrown doubt on the once-accepted theory that these Indian cultures had flourished without any outside influences.

Whatever the answer to this riddle, there came a time when foreigners arrived on the shores of Mexico—in the early sixteenth century. However, for centuries before their coming, the Valley of Mexico in the Central Plateau was dominated first by Toltecs and then by Nahua-speaking tribes, as the south of Mexico was by the Maya and Zapotec people. About 1000 A.D. the Mixtecs overcame the Zapotecs of Oaxaca, built their City of the Dead at Mitla, took over Monte Albán, and intermingled with other powerful tribes. They became master metallurgists and worked with unrivaled skill in gold and silver. In Michoacán the Tarascans were building a powerful empire extending northward.

There are too many tribes to treat of in any detail, including the Olmec, Toltec, and Chichimec tribes, which arrived successively during the early Christian era and eventually established a capital at Texcoco on a lake in the Valley of Mexico. These tribes paid little heed at first to a new and savage tribe of wanderers that offered human sacrifices (like the Chichimecs) to their chief god, called Mexitli or Huitzilopochtli, and were known as Aztecs or Mexicans. This tribe settled on a lake in the Valley of Mexico, where they saw the omen that had been promised by their soothsayers when they began their long journey—an eagle perched on a cactus with a serpent in its beak, now the symbol of Mexico. About 1325, they founded a city on the lake and named it Tenochtitlán.

Within a century the Mexicans or Aztecs had absorbed the skills and lore of their more civilized neighbors and through their ferocity had become so powerful that they exacted tribute and sacrifices from many conquered tribes. It was not an empire as Europeans understood the term, because it never had a centralized government that incorporated other dominions and governed them. It held subject tribes only by constant threat of new warfare and retaliation. The Mexicans were the most feared power in the land far beyond the Valley of Mexico.

Picture Tenochtitlán as it must have been in its prime, a city of nearly 300,000. It was a city of white towers and temples and lines of causeways set in the blue lake waters. It was populous and clean, full of trees, gardens, fruits, and tropical flowers and fragrance. The edges of the city were bordered with man-made islands on rafts on which grew plants and trees that by their roots anchored the rafts to the lake bottoms (like those seen at Xochimilco near the capital today). White-clad farmers poled dugouts through the canals to cultivate their gardens. On some islands thatch-roofed houses were built.

Over the broad causeways passed city people, countrymen, and merchants from afar with produce, crafts, and tools for the markets. Canoes floated through the canals laden with flowers, metalwork, textiles, and food. All transport was by boat or bearers.

Toward the markets and temples the crowds grew denser. Priests walked by in black robes, their hair lank, blood-stained, and tangled from sacrificial ceremonies. Clan leaders and nobles dressed in rich mantles of featherwork and fine textiles woven and painted "after the fashion of Moorish draperies," writes Cortés. The common women wore highly colored robes reaching from the waist to the feet. Women of high rank wore "bodices of fine cotton, very loose fitting, cut and embroidered after the fashion of the vestment worn by [Spanish] bishops and abbots," with flowers adorning their hair. Merchants were trailed by clerks, warriors, apprentices, and carriers. Some warriors wore armor of colored padded cotton and helmets shaped like the heads of jaguars, wolves, or eagles.

As is still true today, each product had its special place in the market. And, as now, they were arranged in pleasing geometric or patterned displays—ripe red tomatoes and dark-green chiles flanking yellow squashes, green avocados, and yellow oranges in neat piles. There were fruits, pottery, articles of clothing, weapons, tools, basketry, cloaks, tiaras, and rugs of featherwork. In another section was game, dead or alive—turkey, pheasant, partridge, rabbit, hare, deer, wild fowl, and the squat hairless dog bred for food. Except for cocoa beans or pieces of tin, which served as primitive currency, everything was bartered. A noble lady might offer feathers dusted with gold for a large rug, or a priest pieces of metal for a new cotton cloak.

There was a slave quarter too. Some slaves were captured warriors kept in chains. Some were paying off a
debt in slavery for having stolen or destroyed property.
Others were children sold into slavery by their parents,
who could no longer support them. They would learn
a trade and later be freed by the substitution of a younger
brother or sister. Or a father might sell himself for a
period of slavery. Slaves were generally well protected
and treated. No one was born a slave; the children of a
slave were free. Slaves could buy their own freedom
and even own others. Slaves lost eligibility for public
office and their civil rights, but little more.

Above the finer houses of stone reared the truncated
pyramids, fearsome and majestic, the apex, the pride, and
the horror of this epoch. It was here before the squat
god Huitzilopochtli, made of stone set with seed pearls,
gold, jade, and turquoise, that victims were sacrificed—
not singly or in small groups as in previous generations
but by the hundreds and even thousands, while the great
drum throbbed out doom. The walls of the temple were
blackened with blood, lined with knives, conch-shell
trumpets, banners, and baskets of human hearts. On
ceremonial days the grim procession mounted the steep
114 steps, seemingly vanished into the sky at each terraced level, and reappeared on the next steps. One by
one the victims were seized by the priests and lifted to
the sacrificial stone. Here the priest cut deep with an
obsidian knife, snatched out the beating heart, offered it
to the sun, and cast it at the feet of the idol.

Yet the cleanliness of the people amazed foreigners.
A thousand street cleaners kept the streets in order.
There were public baths and toilets. Every day fresh

water was piped in to the city by aqueduct, with spare ducts that could be used when the main conduit was being cleaned.

The foregoing were the tangibles of Aztec life, from the gracious and beautiful to the grotesque and repellent. The intangibles lay in the social and religious structure. Education was primarily by imitation. The boys were trained by their fathers in arts, crafts, carpentry, agriculture, and the girls by their mothers in weaving, spinning, cookery, and the household arts. Children up to six years did minor chores and learned the use of household tools.

Boys were urged to be honest and upright because dishonesty and theft would defile them. Girls were adjured to speak low, walk with downcast eyes, and be modest. Parents usually were gentle and kind and used admonition for discipline—up to the age of eight. After that, a misbehaving child was rigorously punished. For minor misdeeds his hand might be painfully pricked with a maguey spine. For misbehavior of any magnitude, he might even be left bound and exposed overnight on a mountain. The heaviness of the responsibility of assuming adult chores so early in childhood was balanced by the satisfaction of playing an adult and respected role in the home and community.

There was always the incentive of being able to rise through energy, skill, and creative work to a high rank as priest, warrior, merchant, counselor, or craftsman. (In the Inca society of South America, on the other hand, a child was born or assigned to a definite role from which there was little or no departure.) Boys of fifteen or older attended a "house of youth" to study civics, arts and crafts, history, religious observance, and the techniques of war.

Some continued to study for priestly and chiefly duties in a sort of seminary. Some girls were trained as priestesses. Others specialized in weaving, featherwork, or a comparable skill. The girls were considered marriageable by sixteen and the boys by twenty.

Polygamy was practiced by the upper classes, and divorce was allowed for physical mistreatment or failure to support and educate the children. Women had more personal than legal influence but were permitted to rule as regent for a son on occasion. The children of a high-ranking man benefited from his position but could themselves reach a like status only through equivalent service. Superior skill in farming, hunting, crafts, or war was honored and might lead to representation at the tribal council and eventually to chieftainship. Some men of great experience and wisdom were selected to teach in the house of youth. Others kept records for the clan storehouses, distributed communal property, and even traveled to collect tributes from other tribes.

The economic base of the Aztec society was communal ownership of productive property, but private wealth existed. It was nevertheless a democratic society in which position had to be earned. Leaders were often chosen from the same noble families, but they had first to undergo the tests for eminence. Priests worked closely with civil leaders and were also powerful. The immediate steps to supreme chief and religious leader were four offices that controlled military forces, maintained order among the clans, and settled disputes beyond the solution of the clan. Heading the government of internal affairs was an officer, always male, though known as the Snake Woman. Any of these leaders could be deposed for unsatisfactory performance.

Although the Aztecs generally applied the principle of restitution rather than punishment of a sinner or criminal, there were exceptions. Whoever endangered the community was exiled or killed. A thief was enslaved or fined double the amount stolen, half for the person robbed, half for the public treasury. Pilfering in the market led to death by stoning, and the crime of murder brought death. Drunkenness was not tolerated except that old people were exempted from punishment for it. There was little or no imprisonment for crime—but there was comparatively little crime.

Even in a city of the size of Tenochtitlán, large for either Europe or the Americas, there was little conflict. The people were strongly community-minded and were well served by the community. They had faith in it. Although Aztec law was brutal in extremes, it was a rare individual who violated the social code and paid the price. Captured warriors in most cases were sacrificed, but since their own people often practiced both human sacrifice and cannibalism, they were prone to be resigned rather than horrified by their fate. It was believed that the victor could thus absorb the strength and cunning of the captive.

It was a society that lived in harmony with its environment, not yet devastated by erosion and deforestation, and most citizens found rewards in their skills and the esteem of family and community. The Valley of Mexico abounded with fowl and deer. It was fertile with natural resources, blue with salt and freshwater lakes and lagoons, ringed with mountains jutting up 10,000 feet high, topped by pine forests and by towering volcanoes to the south-east. It was certainly one of the most beautiful regions of the world.

But the culture of the Aztecs did *not* represent the zenith of the Indian civilizations. It was a step down from those of some of its predecessors and neighbors. Aztec art, architecture, and pottery, their calendar, and their glyphs were inferior. Aztec bloodthirstiness and greed were oppressive and carried the seeds of their downfall. There were rumors of evil omens and prophecies. The King of Texcoco, convinced by his soothsayers that strangers would one day rule the Aztec lands, staked his kingdom against three turkey cocks on the outcome of a ritualistic ball game with Moctezuma II, Emperor of the Aztecs—and won three of the five games in token of the justice of these prophecies.

The stage was set for one of the most dramatic events in history.

3

The Conquest and New Spain

In the year 1519, a Spanish adventurer in his thirties, named Hernán Cortés, landed with eleven ships on the east coast of Mexico from Cuba. He had been sent there by Governor Velásquez of Cuba for the sake of God, glory, and gold. With him disembarked 110 sailors, 553 soldiers, a couple of hundred Indian servants from the islands, cannon—and sixteen horses. One of his men, Bernal Díaz de Castillo, has left us a fascinating, richly detailed account of the entire conquest, including a description of the horses. In his *Chronicles*, he says, for example, that there was "a light chestnut horse with three white feet, which wasn't any good," and "an excellent light chestnut horse and fast," and "a very good dark horse called El Arriero."

On the pretext that most of the ships were no longer seaworthy, Cortés had them stripped of useful items, like sails, and burned. He said that any who wanted to return to Cuba on the single remaining ship could do so. That shamed any who felt reluctant and left them no alternative but to follow him against the might of Mexico.

How could this handful of Spaniards conquer a vast domain of seven to nine million hostile Indians who were fierce and brave warriors with thorough knowledge of their country?

The story is complex. Legend and superstition, superior arms, armor, and discipline, the immense advantage of horses, and the peculiar political structure and military customs of the Aztec domain played a part. So did several thousand Indian allies. And so did an astonishingly adroit young Indian princess, Malintzín or La Malinche. Many of the tribes in the hinterlands resisted for centuries or were never conquered. Even today there remain a few pockets of Indian tribes in the mountains or jungles who have had virtually no contact with civilization, like the Lacandones of the south.

The Aztecs were the key to the riddle. They dominated much of Mexico, made slaves or sacrifices of thousands of prisoners from defeated tribes, demanded provisions and tribute, and sent their arrogant agents to supervise these transactions. Naturally the subject tribes were restive and eager to revolt under auspicious circumstances. Also, in the Indian tradition of war, battles ceased when a chief was captured or slain, and war operations were suspended to allow for harvesting and agricultural chores. Protracted war was unknown. The omens for several years had foretold disaster. Moctezuma had verbal and pictorial reports from his couriers about the first landing of the invaders, but he lapsed into a state of fatal indecision, unable to determine whether to pacify or resist.

The arrival of the Spaniards revived the legend that one day Quetzalcoatl of the fair skin, blue eyes, and beard would return to his people to bring peace and prosperity. The rumor spread that the foreign captain might be the god himself.

Bernal Díaz has left word pictures of the principal actors in the drama—Moctezuma, Cortés, and La Malinche—

and the pictorial reporters of the Aztecs portrayed them in their codices. These codices were historical forerunners of comic strips.

Moctezuma was about forty, says Díaz, "of good height, well proportioned, and slender. . . . His face was a little long, but pleasant, while his eyes were attractive, and he showed in his person and in his glance both affection and, when necessary, seriousness. He was most clean, bathing every day."

Then came Hernán Cortés. He had studied law briefly, had enlisted in an expedition from Spain to the New World. He distinguished himself in the campaign to subjugate Cuba and was made the Governor's secretary and the King's treasurer. When Governor Velásquez decided to equip an expedition to the mainland, Cortés, not long married, was appointed leader. When rumor reached him that the Governor had changed his mind, he simply bolted before anyone else could be appointed.

Bernal Díaz describes him as of good height, strongly made, somewhat pale of complexion, serious in expression. "His beard and hair were black and thin. His chest and shoulders were broad. His legs were bowed and he was an excellent horseman. . . . He was congenial with his men, something of a poet, and wrote well. . . ."

He was pious and headstrong, but a master diplomat, an opportunist of the first magnitude, a brilliant tactician and strategist, a man of resource and imagination. He knew the value of a sudden swift stroke followed by leniency or severity according to the occasion. He had courage, vision, eloquence, tenacity, and a high sense of drama and knew how to command the deference and ardor of his men. When the Indians mistook him for Quetzalcoatl, he played the role of an immortal. He exploited the thunder of cannon and the Indians' fear of horse and rider as a single terrifying man-beast like the Centaur. And he had the wisdom to pacify those tribes that were peaceably inclined by presents of beads, bells, Castilian shirts —and by fair treatment.

After the first battle with the Tabasco Indians of the coast, the conquered chief presented Cortés with gold diadems, masks, earrings, cloth, and trinkets—and twenty Indian girls. It was one of these girls, La Malinche—known after her baptism as Doña Marina—"of good appearance, intelligent and poised," who became a legend in her own right and a symbol of the union of Indian and Spaniard.

The manner and bearing of this teen-aged girl must have suggested something of her history. Bernal Díaz thought she must be the daughter of great chiefs and the mistress of slaves. She was. When her father died, her mother remarried, and to ensure the position of the child of her second marriage, she sold her firstborn into slavery. Malintzín was brought to the east coast as a slave.

After her baptism as Doña Marina, Cortés gave her to one of his favorite officers, but when he found that she knew the language of the Mexicans and the Maya and was learning Spanish rapidly, he recognized her unique value and rearranged matters to his satisfaction. He had an interpreter, a Spaniard who had lived for years among the Indians, but Marina became his interpreter, constant companion, and counselor. In the codices, the picture histories, she is shown at Cortés's side in every campaign and conference. He became known as "the captain of Marina" from being always in her company— or Malinche for short.

Díaz, her fervent admirer, reports that she "had such manly courage that she never allowed us to see any sign of weakness in her, although she heard daily how we were going to be killed and eaten with chili, and had been around after battles when we were all wounded and sick." More than once her advice saved the Spaniards—notably from an ambush in Cholula—and without her services the Conquest might never have succeeded. She was beloved by Indians and Spaniards alike because she constantly intervened on behalf of her people, though her loyalty to Cortés never wavered. Now the word *malinchismo* refers to lovers of foreigners.

Then came the sequences of feints, battles and plots, the wounds, losses, and heartaches; the agonizing sight of heads and limbs dismembered from Spanish corpses and tossed tauntingly back into the Spanish camp; the suffering from cold, exposure, and hunger on the mountains; the weary journeys, ambushes, and narrow escapes. When the little band of soldiers reached the summit of the mountain pass overlooking the Valley of Mexico on a brilliant November day of 1519, they were stunned at the sight below them. Not even Venice, that jewel of Europe, could match the splendor and beauty of Tenochtitlán.

Almost as impressive was the encounter with Moctezuma. Wavering between war and friendship, fear and pride, he advanced from the city to meet them borne on a litter beneath a marvelously worked canopy of green feathers, gold, silver, and pearls. When he stepped down, nobles walked before him to sweep the ground and lay tapestries so that his feet, sandaled with gold and precious gems, need not touch the earth.

Cortés dismounted from his horse, addressed Mocte-

zuma through Marina, and gave him a necklace of glass
stones strung on a golden cord. It was small return for
the extraordinary presents Moctezuma had so mistakenly
sent in the hope of turning the newcomers away—gifts
of wheels of solid gold and silver worked in relief, animals fashioned in gold, handsome necklaces, fine cloth,
and featherwork. These had only whetted the Spanish
appetite and determination to reach the source of these
riches. The Spaniards, said Cortés wittily, suffered from
a disease of the heart for which gold was the only specific.

Moctezuma led the company to great halls with a can-
opied bed for each soldier, with walls whitewashed and
adorned with fragrant branches. Moctezuma gave Cortés
a rich golden collar and himself placed it around his neck
and said, "Malinche, this house is yours and your brothers'. Rest."

Within weeks Moctezuma was a prisoner in his own
capital! Within two years that splendid city was razed,
Moctezuma dead, and his valiant successor Cuauhtémoc
the captive of the conquerors. The Spaniards had van-
quished the Aztecs and succeeded them as rulers of the
land!

Moctezuma seemed invulnerable. In his palace he dined
behind a gilded wooden screen, while hundreds ate in the
great hall. Four beautiful women brought basins of water
and towels for washing, spread white cloths and napkins
on a low table. They and various nobles offered dishes
from which Moctezuma selected the choicest—wild pig,
quail, duck, rabbit, seafood brought by runner from the
coast, venison, pigeons. From cups of gold he drank

beverages unknown to the newcomers, frothing chocolate or the pulque drawn from the maguey cactus.

All who entered his presence had to divest themselves
of rich clothing and come in barefoot, bareheaded, and
clean, with downcast eyes. Yet Moctezuma was regally
simple in manner and most thoughtful in providing gifts
and supplies for his unwanted guests. He and Cortés
professed the deepest respect and affection for each other,
but each was wary.

The first conflict came when the Spaniards visited the
main temple of the city. Offended and horrified by the
ugly sights, Cortés derided the Indian gods and tried to
convert Moctezuma to Christianity. With dignity his host
rejected these efforts and made offerings to his gods to
atone for the insults and indignities. Yet with tolerance
he permitted the visitors to build their own chapel to a
foreign god.

Moctezuma's generosity notwithstanding, Cortés knew
his position was perilous and took a step as audacious as
his burning of the ships on landing to make the Mexican
expedition imperative. On hearing news of a battle between a small group of Spaniards left on the coast at
Veracruz and some Mexican forces, he marched with an
escort to the palace, charged Moctezuma with disloyalty
to their "friendship," and announced that he would pardon
such treachery only if the Emperor surrendered himself
as hostage. Marina urged Moctezuma to capitulate to
avoid a revolt. Unresisting but with tears in his eyes, the
chief came with Cortés as prisoner.

The jealous Governor of Cuba sent forces to capture
the all too successful Cortés. Leaving his lieutenant

Alvarado in charge of Tenochtitlán, Cortés led some of his men back to the coast and with consummate skill battled and then recruited the very forces sent to capture him, including some more horses. But in his absence, Alvarado had massacred the Aztec celebrants at a feast he had given them leave to hold. When the triumphant Captain returned with his reinforcements of men and horses, he found the city in a turmoil of revolt.

Beleaguered and desperate after attacks in which Moctezuma had died from stoning by his own embittered people, the Spaniards and their Indian allies constructed a portable bridge to enable them to escape from the heart of the city across the canals and causeways. Cortés divided the treasures among his men and quietly led them out in darkness to escape. But the alarm was sounded, and instantly the lake and canals filled with enemy warriors in canoes, and the city and lake were bloodied with corpses. Hundreds of Spaniards, too greedy to lose the gold, which weighed them down, drowned in the lakes or were overtaken and killed by the Mexicans. Only twenty-three horses and a few bands of Spaniards escaped.

This was the *Noche Triste*, the sad night on which the Conquest seemed doomed. In five days over 800 Spaniards and 1,200 Tlaxcalan allies were lost. Only 500 Spaniards survived.

Yet Cortés made more ammunition, using sulphur from the crater of Popocatépetl, made cannon, built brigs to give him control of the lakes, and so heartened his army that he came back to besiege Tenochtitlán. He razed it building by building, in spite of a bitter defense, and captured the city and its ruler Cuauhtémoc on August

13, 1521. Mexico became *Nueva España,* a colony of the Spanish Empire.

Whose conquest was it? Did Spain truly succeed in imposing its culture, religion, architecture, and art on the new lands, or did the native population remain Indian to the core? Or instead of either, was the foreign culture absorbed by the patient Indians and transformed into something distinct from either source, bearing the imprint of both cultures?

In Mexico the Indian has survived disease, slavery, and slaughter, the imposition of a foreign god and culture, the systematic effort to obliterate his own. The legacy of Mexico is one of massacre, assassination, conspiracy, sacrifice, ruthless egoism, religious and antireligious frenzy —and toil.

There are some noteworthy differences in the settlement of North and Latin America.

The Northern colonies were settled in the main by sober middle-class men *and their families.* They came to escape religious or civil persecution and with intent to *colonize.* They expected to farm, work, and make new homes, not seek glory, religious conversions, or gold. The Indians were variously regarded with indifference, tolerance, hostility, and friendliness, sometimes as allies, sometimes as enemies. They were constantly pushed by battle or treaties farther and farther from their homelands. They did not number more than a million when the settlers came, never developed a high culture. There were some missionary efforts, but the colonists were more concerned with establishing their own religious beliefs (often intolerant) and churches. Most of them came with some regard for self-government and some experience with its problems. The main elements of the British colonies were respectable and hard-working.

The Spaniards, on the other hand, came of a people isolated in the Iberian peninsula who had for centuries warred with the invading Moors and been subjected to foreign rule. With the liberation of Spain from the Moors in the fifteenth century, the warrior was the most admired and honored of men, the most likely to find fame and fortune. The farmer was scorned. Hence menial work was despised by the Spaniards and in New Spain was considered fit only for the natives. A grant of land was not enough. Indians must be added to work the land and mines that the Spaniards acquired. Individualism and license were the earmarks of the conquerors.

They were men bred to warfare, of aggressive personality and ambition, sometimes of high birth but more often not, and rarely men of education. Wives were left behind. There is little mention of Spanish women in the early years.

During three colonial centuries, from 1519 to 1810, only 300,000 Spaniards emigrated to Mexico, whereas by 1776 the American colonies had a population of about 3,000,000. Some of the adventurers married Spanish-born wives and brought them to Mexico. Their offspring were the *criollos* (Creoles), the Mexican-born Spaniards. Most took Indian wives, and the product of such unions was the mestizo, a blend of Indian with Spanish and Moorish blood. A strict caste system evolved—the Spaniard, rich with lands, Indians, and offices; the criollo, restricted to minor offices and more limited opportunities and wealth, probably because there was some feeling on the part of native-born Spaniards that colonials were inferior; the mestizo, who performed menial tasks or served as a tradesman or a small businessman; and the Indian, who was ignored except as the lowest of menial workers, in effect a slave.

The difference in attitude toward sex counted heavily. In Spain there had been much mixing of Spanish and Moorish blood. Intermarriage and interbreeding were accepted, as were the hybrid children. In colonial New England, on the contrary, miscegenation was frowned upon, and the man who fathered half-Indian children usually disowned them, while in Latin America an Indian wife and her children had a certain accepted status and were relatively well treated. Cortés sired a son named Martín by his Spanish wife and another, also named Martín, by Marina.

So the racial lines were blended instead of separated, and the Latin-American world was gradually dominated by this fusion. It was the mestizo who became the unwitting instrument of the spread of the Spanish language, and this served to unify Latin America in culture.

The Spaniards found in Mexico alone an estimated populace of at least 5,000,000 and probably closer to 9,000,000 Indians. Many of them were in an advanced stage of culture, stable, settled in large and beautiful cities, with a background of centuries of religious and civil history, many with a literature, art, architecture, and musical tradition of high merit.

Besides the differences in attitude toward sex and toward manual labor and the difference in the size of population and of cultural level of the natives, there was another important factor in Latin America—the powerful impetus

of seeking converts for the glory of God and the Catholic
Church. "God, Glory, and Gold" was always the cry of
the Spanish Conquest, though as the decades wore on, it
was gold that became foremost—gold, silver, precious
stones, and the wealth of land and slaves. The original
influx of churchmen filled with altruism, humanity, and
foresight soon petered out into church servants ranging
from good and mediocre to downright vicious.

At first the friars came as missionaries devoted to con-
version of souls and the betterment of the natives. Even
Cortés knelt to kiss the hems of their garments when
the first friars walked the 300 miles from Veracruz to
Mexico City. His genuine religious ardor greatly promoted the cause of Christianity among the natives. The
rest was accomplished by the wisdom of the early friars
and the vacuum left by the destruction and disparage-
ment of native temples and idols.

To the conquerors, less interested in humanitarian considerations and religious motives, the friars became trou-
blemakers because they defended the Indians and tried
to enforce regulations for their welfare. Fray Bartolomé
de las Casas, a Dominican friar (1474-1566) who wrote
The Destruction of the Indies, protested most violently
against abuse of the Indians and compiled volumes on
the atrocities perpetrated by the gentry and some members of the clergy. In his ardor, Fray Bartolomé greatly
exaggerated slaughter by the Spaniards and minimized
the human sacrifices of the pre-Conquest period to a
mere 50 or so victims a year. He claimed that *after* the
Conquest the Spaniards had killed about 12,000,000 Indians—a greater number than actually inhabited all of Mex-

ico—and accused a single Spanish soldier of killing 10,000 Indians with his lance in one hour.

It is true that vicious and greedy men like Nuño de Guzmán and his followers killed, raped, enslaved, and destroyed to a horrifying degree and achieved such power that it took years for the royal authorities to master them. Guzmán was an enemy of Cortés and in the late 1520's President of the Audiencia, a council appointed by the Spanish crown to rule and act as a court of justice over the colonials. It is also true that Spanish-borne diseases like smallpox exterminated the natives by the hundreds of thousands and even by millions. Without doubt many of the Spaniards, both secular and religious, gravely abused the Indians. Many of them were fearfully overworked, underfed, deprived of shelter and sufficient clothing, taken from their families, whipped and maltreated, forced to work in mines or on the land at great distances from their homes, and not cared for in sickness. In some cases whole villages of people were uprooted and marched with too little food and rest to build a church or hacienda at whatever cost of lives and suffering.

Eventually the New Laws of 1542 were passed for the protection of the Indians, but they were too advanced and unpopular in the colonics to be properly enforced. They served only to mitigate some of the worst abuses.

Yet in most instances the natives, long accustomed to donating services and giving tribute to Aztec masters, tolerated the practice of service. Sometimes they became so devoted that they resisted a change of mission. There was never a sudden cleavage between a primitive paradise and the advent of the Spaniards. In Aztec times the average Indian lived a cleaner, better-nourished, and more healthful life, perhaps, but the good life was always reserved for a very few at the top. Mexican history has always—until recently—been a shift of master and regime: Aztecs . . . conquerors . . . the friars . . . the *encomenderos* (owners of vast lands) . . . the viceroys and bishops.

The churchmen have a curiously mixed record. In doing what they conceived to be their duty, they destroyed pagan temples, idols, fine architecture, artwork, and historical and literary records, to replace them with Catholic edifices and shrines. Fray Diego de Landa burned the codex scrolls of the Maya—only three are known to have escaped destruction! Yet this same Bishop Landa learned the language of the Maya and wrote a *Relación de las Cosas de Yucatán* (Relation of the Things of Yucatán), which preserves many details of the customs, life, and history of the Maya. Bernardino de Sahagún also destroyed precious codices, but he learned the dialects and history of the Aztecs and wrote a dictionary and history. Ironically, Archbishop Zumárraga was probably innocent of the burning of manuscripts of which he was accused.

Fray Pedro de Gante adroitly made use of the Indian love of dancing and singing in religious fiestas to adapt stories from the Bible for instructing his native pupils. This example was followed so fervently and indiscriminately that soon all kinds of elements became incongruously mixed, to the uncritical delight of Indians and less learned padres. Alexander the Great, Christ, the Moors, assorted saints, and the Virgin, as well as some pagan leftovers, are today all lumped together in a glorious hodgepodge. But it has worked. The natives readily transferred their allegiance or adapted the new holy figures for use in their own religion. Hence the many brown-skinned

Madonnas and saints with whom they feel more comfortable.

The Indians in Gante's school, located first in Texcoco and later in the capital, learned Spanish, painting, music, arts, and crafts. The most promising ones even learned reading, writing, and Latin. Toribio de Benavente (Motolinía, "the ragged one") wrote a fascinating history of New Spain. Bishop Vasco de Quiroga founded a mission in Tzintzuntzan and won over the hostile Indians of Michoacán by patience, kindness, and understanding and by his faith that the natives could equal or surpass the Europeans. He built schools, taught Spanish arts and crafts and agricultural methods, and made craft centers of various villages.

In all Mexico there is no statue in honor of Cortés nor any street or town named after him, although in his own time he was revered and loved by both Indians and Spaniards. No conquest is free of atrocities, but among the conquerors Cortés was the most enlightened and farsighted, an epitome of the best, with the virtues and faults of his era.

It is not surprising that mestizo Mexico wishes to resurrect some great Indian ancestor, and it is fashionable now to exalt Cuauhtémoc as hero and to play down the contributions of Cortés and the Spaniards. Cuauhtémoc was heroic in defending his people and later in resisting the torture applied by the Spaniards to make him disclose the site of Aztec treasures. (To the chief at his side who implored him for permission to end the torture by confessing the secret, he said scornfully, "You see *I* am on no bed of roses either," and pointed at the hot coals applied to his feet.) He was later taken with Cortés on the march to Honduras and there executed in the belief, founded or not, that he was plotting an uprising. But it should be granted that the Spaniards, especially Cortés and some of the padres, also made invaluable contributions to the shaping of Mexico as a nation.

From the beginning Cortés sought to establish friendly relations with each tribe, and when successful, he dealt with them justly. He once strung up one of his soldiers for stealing turkeys from a native. The example was force- ful—even though at the behest of friends Cortés allowed the man to be cut down and saved—and his men were under strict discipline throughout his campaigns. Away from his influence it was sometimes a different story.

He was not above double dealing to achieve his ends. When tax collectors from Moctezuma came to the "fat chief" of Cempoal to demand twenty sacrificial victims, Cortés, to impress the chief with his strength and justice, commanded him to give no further tribute and ordered the collectors to be imprisoned. Then secretly he released two of them to report that the chief was responsible for this impudence and that he personally was friendly to Moctezuma.

But as a rule, he used drastic measures only under duress, when he suspected treason or ambush. In Cholula when a friendly Indian woman invited Marina to take shelter with her to escape the coming ambush, Marina disclosed the plan to Cortés. He turned the tables on the Indians by massacring those who had gathered to kill the foreign- ers.

He antagonized his own men by unfair division of loot –human and material—but he commanded their love and respect by sharing their trials, hazards, chores, and even by standing watch with them. His ardor and example buoyed them up against impossible odds, and he pacified them in their grumblings. "God gave him such grace that to whatsoever he turned his hand he did well, especially in pacifying the nations and peoples of those parts," reports Bernal Díaz.

He was builder as well as soldier. Though he destroyed Tenochtitlán, he raised another city in its stead and peopled it with 30,000 families. They were granted, he wrote to the Emperor in 1524, "such liberties and immunities that they would increase greatly. They live quite as they please, and many artisans make a living among the Spaniards. . . ." He asked that all ships bring plants, seeds, and provisions that would be useful in the colonies. He established hospitals, built palaces, supported the church generously, and continued explorations. He built a fleet, explored the coasts, and sent products to Peru, imported cattle, sheep and other animals, planted wheat, sugarcane, and fruit trees, and encouraged silk culture.

He opposed giving estates and slaves to his soldiers—and then helped himself to the biggest slice of all. Within 50 years over 500 *encomiendas* (vast estates) had been granted to individuals, encompassing the best farmland of the country. But unlike most landholders, Cortés did have some regard for the welfare of the Indians.

Despite this, it was urgent for the Spanish government to break the power of the conquerors and replace it with civil power. The King delegated this task to the Audiencia and to his Viceroy, proxy for the King. Desperate over the consistent blocking of his plans and activities, Cortés returned to Spain to appeal to the King (his second re-

turn) and died there in 1547. By his request his body was
sent to Mexico for burial.

Someday there will be fuller acknowledgment of the
debts owed, despite slaughter and destruction, to Cortés
and the Spanish heritage. That will be another stride on the
path to national maturity and a clearer perspective.

Besides the missions and encomiendas, which diffused
Spanish culture and power, the towns united native and
Spanish customs and became symbols of Spain. Around
each central plaza were built a municipal palace, a military
headquarters and arsenal, and usually the main church and
marketplace. By preference both Spaniards and Indians
lived in towns rather than on isolated farms, and people
went out daily from their homes to work the land. Most
towns sprang up in fertile regions, near mines or good
harbors, and in a healthful climate. Nearby would be an
ejido, communal land used for grazing, threshing, slaughter, beehives, and other public needs. Not far from the
towns were Indian villages to supply services for the
Spaniards. Reached only occasionally by a traveler or
friar were those tribes that were never conquered or absorbed into a Spanish dominion.

Haciendas and encomiendas were villages in themselves,
self-sustaining, with carpenters, masons, bakers, farmers,
shopkeepers, smiths, and tradesmen. The plantations of
our Old South are the closest thing we know to such es-
tablishments.

Most important of all was the capital. The contrast between it and the shining city of Tenochtitlán did not reflect
credit on the Spaniards. The Indian city had been im-
maculately kept, with provisions for sanitation. In Spanish

colonial times, muck and garbage created an intolerable stench and promoted epidemics of smallpox, diphtheria, typhoid, bubonic plague, yellow fever, measles, and rabies.

Yet the capital was a city of beauty and grandeur, in 1612 measuring eight miles in circumference. The buildings were of volcanic *tezontle*, a reddish stone, porous, light, and easy to work. Streets were wide and straight, crossing on bridges many channels from the lake. Daily 1,000 boats and 3,000 mules brought provisions to the 145,000 inhabitants—of whom only 15,000 were Spanish. There were richly appointed churches and convents, all of which maintained schools. Santo Domingo, the largest church community, had over 200 friars, many highly educated and fine preachers, and was perhaps unequaled in Spain itself. But even then the city had begun to sink because of its swampy foundations.

At first, what education there was stemmed from the priests and church schools. Girls received almost none except in housekeeping and religious matters. Indians, except for a few lads of promise, were almost ignored. Boys and young men of good families were sent to Europe for an education.

The University of Mexico was chartered in 1551, thirty years after the Conquest. Courses included canon law, sacred writings, native languages, Latin, classical authors, grammar, and eventually medicine, which was earlier considered the lowly province of the Indians. Research was circumscribed, and few scholars undertook any investigation frowned on by the Church—and the Church frowned on much. No professors or students of significant stature emerged. The heresy that sometimes sprang up in the equally theological colleges of North America and

helped to encourage the flowering of New England was
conspicuously absent.

Juan Pablos had brought the first printing press to the
New World in the 1530's, but nearly all books printed
were religious and of low literary standards. Those children who were schooled had to bring their own texts
from home—lives of the saints or romances of chivalry.
Primary textbooks were rare.

The chasm between the Indian and the Creole or Spanish
aristocracy widened when the silver baronies developed.
So rich were the silver barons who exploited the mines
that some of their horses were bridled and shod with silver.
One grandee paved the street between the church and
his mansion with silver for the wedding of his daughter.
In 1625, when coaches were almost unknown in the American colonies, there were reportedly 15,000 in Mexico
City. These magnificent vehicles were drawn by mule or
horse teams through hordes of wretched thieves, beggars,
and ruffians who formed the bulk of the inhabitants of the
city.

Although Cortés had been made the Marqués del
Valle de Oaxaca on his first triumphal return to Spain,
the Crown had already begun a policy of easing the
conquerors out of authority. By degrees a civil government took over. The ruling body for the new colonies,
the Council of the Indies, had at first made the incredibly
ill-judged choice of Nuño de Guzmán, who had instigated
a reign of terror. He so aroused the hatred of the Indians
by his violence that they began a desperate rebellion.

Five men of strict probity were chosen as the second
Audiencia of Mexico. They cleaned up the mess left by

Guzmán, but it took a long time to get rid of him. Wisely they granted to Indian communities the right of self-government and justice under their own elected officers. The native chiefs thus became officers of the Crown. They were given salaries, privileges, and immunities and formed an Indian nobility of sorts.

When New Spain was made a Viceroyalty in 1535, the first proxy of the Crown was Don Antonio de Mendoza. He aimed to undermine the feudal power of the conquerors and to centralize authority. He protected the Indians, raised the royal revenues, policed the country. He encouraged mining, agriculture, commerce and trade. He checkmated Cortés and other factions, built cities, roads, and public services. He handled the grandiose assignment masterfully and put down a rebellion by the Indians. By the end of his rule, Spanish power was set firmly to weather the next three centuries.

In the regime of his successor, Don Luis de Velasco, the revised New Laws engineered the freeing of the Indian slaves. Such reforms were practical as well as humanitarian, and this emancipation went through despite a decline in royal revenue.

Along the line of viceroys were scoundrels and weaklings, but most were capable and zealous men. One of the most revered was the second Revillagigedo, who ruled in New Spain from 1789 to 1795. He was known as a great reformer and statesman.

While New Spain grew in glory and architectural splendor, the baroque flowered extravagantly in such famous structures as José de la Borda's Church of Santa Prisca in Taxco and the fine cathedral at Puebla.

Less glorious was the Spanish Inquisition. Its purpose

in Mexico was to consolidate the Catholic faith and eliminate troublesome minorities of Jews, Lutherans, Protestants who had been shipwrecked there, and other heretics, although it was forbidden to molest the natives in New Spain. The methods devised included torture by rack and wheel, fire and water. Guilt by association penalized many innocent people among the friends and families of the victims. Only forty-three persons were executed by the Inquisition in New Spain (more than that died during the New England witchcraft panic)—but that figure takes no account of the hundreds who were imprisoned, tortured, or more mildly mistreated.

The Inquisition was not the only scourge of New Spain. Another was the squandering of the forests of the country for fuel and building, so that areas long forested were denuded. This led to one of the most appalling problems of today—the wasting of the land through erosion by wind and water. The importation of sheep, in some respects a boon, hastened the erosion because the sheep cropped the grass so close as to ruin vast acreages.

Silver, gold, and other riches poured out of the country and stayed briefly in the royal coffers of Spain or in the pirate ships of England. As was the case in most colonial empires, New Spain was forbidden to trade with any but Spanish ports, excluding all ports in the Western Hemisphere. Mexican manufactures were prohibited. All enterprises in the colonies were discouraged except those that might enrich the mother country.

But gradually Mexico was shaping into an entity despite the history of generations of regionalism, factionalism, and repression. A common religion of Catholicism, however diluted by paganism; a common language, Spanish;

and eventually a dominant group of people, the mestizos, all promoted a growing sense of identification. The short-sighted policy of trying to keep a new and enormous colony dependent upon Spain was to result in revolution.

For three centuries New Spain was the largest and most lustrous jewel in the Spanish crown. But in the nineteenth century the jewel was snatched away.

4

Revolution and Modern Mexico

There are times through the centuries when revolution seems to hang in the air, and it erupts in strange places. In our time it has exploded, for better or worse, in the streets of Budapest, Hungary, and the hills of Cuba. Once it exploded at the walls of a prison in France and before that on a bridge near Concord, Massachusetts, in 1775. And all these events set up reactions.

In Mexico after three hundred years of Spanish rule, revolution erupted in a church in the flat dusty little town of Dolores in 1810. What set the stage for it was the imprisonment in Europe of the Spanish King and his heir, Ferdinand, by Napoleon and the elevation of Joseph Bonaparte to the throne of Spain. An uprising against the viceroy followed in Mexico. With the success of this it became clear that a *coup-d'état* was the natural instrument for a change of government in Mexico. It set a pattern for more than a century of lawlessness.

In 1810 Mexico had a population of 6,000,000 or 7,000,-000 broken into four main groups:

about 15,000 Spaniards of power and wealth at the top
about 500,000 Creoles in less important positions, often merchants or owners of mines and haciendas

about 2,600,000 mestizos of mixed blood, the social out-
casts of the colonial era

3,000,000 to 4,000,000 pure Indians, considered as drones
and little else by Spaniards and Creoles alike.

The intense rivalry between Creole and Spaniard, the frustrations of the mestizo, and the long oppression of the Indian were bound to have a bloody outcome.

Literary clubs and societies looked perfectly innocent
—but under the guise of dancing and card parties, the
members entertained themselves by hatching conspiracies.
One of these was the Literary and Social Club of Querétaro, led by the handsome young Creole, Capt. Ignacio
Allende, commander of the troops at nearby San Miguel
el Grande. Another member was Josefa Ortiz, wife of the
Mayor of Querétaro. A new member recruited by Allende
was the padre of Dolores, lively, middle-aged, scholarly,
and unorthodox Miguel Hidalgo y Costilla. Father Hidalgo
had been censured by his superiors more than once for
unbecoming conduct: reading forbidden books, planting
forbidden grapes and mulberry trees to establish wine
and silk industries, encouraging his parishioners in such
crafts as the making of pottery and tiles—and overindul-
gence in wine, women, cards, and dancing. All these plot-
ters were Creoles who resented the ascendancy and arro-
gance of the Spaniards.

Their aim was not to liberate the peons from bondage
but to end the rule of the envied Spaniards in high office.
At the fair of San Juan de los Lagos, Captain Allende
would proclaim independence from Spain, now ruled by
Bonaparte, in the name of Ferdinand, rightful heir to the
Spanish throne. The country people would join his troops
and eventually the rest of the country. To finance the

insurrection, they would seize Spanish property for the national treasury.

The plot did not work out. It was discovered in September. Sra. Ortiz, locked in a room of her own house, heard of the discovery and sent a messenger to alert Captain Allende in San Miguel. In his absence word was carried to Father Hidalgo on the night of September 15, 1810, while he was playing cards with some friends. Early the next morning he rang the church bells, preached a passionate sermon for freedom to his parishioners, and raised the famous *Grito de Dolores*—the shout for independence and death to the Spaniards.

With a handful of craftsmen, farmers, and jailbirds freed from prison and armed with machetes, hoes, and other tools, he marched toward San Miguel. He stopped en route at the church of Atontonilco to snatch up the banner of the dark Virgin of Guadalupe and then joined forces with Allende's troops in San Miguel. Riot ensued. Realizing the emotional value of a religious leader for the cause of independence, Allende bowed to Hidalgo and was overruled on the need for a small disciplined force rather than an unruly mob—a source of contention that later split the leadership of the revolt.

In a week there were 50,000 in that mob. From the beginning the Indians and mestizos understood only the cry, "Death to the Spaniards," and looted and killed with a vengeance and the approbation of Hidalgo. The worst massacre was in the granary of Guanajuato, where the Spaniards took refuge. Few escaped slaughter.

What started as a Creole rebellion turned into a massive and uncontrollable Indian mayhem. Within months there were dissensions and defeats. The mob melted away. The leaders were captured. Hidalgo was defrocked, all were executed, and the heads of the leaders were stuck on the four corners of the granary in Guanajuato as a terrible warning to rebels.

It was a premature and ill-planned revolt. There was no organization, no concept of a program, no real purpose except to overthrow the Spaniards. Nor was there fertile soil for self-government as there had been in the American colonies in their rebellion against English rule. The background was graft, sale of offices, and the corruption of bosses in small towns and leaders in the capital. Even the Creole sympathizers deserted, horrified by plunder, rapine, and killing. There were no leaders of the integrity and stature of Franklin, Washington, Jefferson, Hamilton, Jay, and Adams.

But the sparks caught fire, and another priest, José María Morelos, took up the cry for independence and led his guerrilla troops with brilliance. He had a program—independence and the partitioning of land among the Indians. Sovereignty was to reside in the people and their elected officials, caste distinctions were to be abolished, and all citizens were to be known as Americans. Laws were to be applied impartially; torture was to be abolished as well as government monopolies. Only skilled mechanics free of political ties would be welcome as foreign residents.

But Morelos too was captured, unfrocked, and in 1815 shot. Unlike Hidalgo, he rejected titles and subordinated himself to civil authorities, but the time was still not ripe. Capable as Morelos was, it was Hidalgo who captured the public fancy and is called the father of modern Mexico.

The nation was in a wretched state. The land was left idle, the best farmers and *hacendados* (estate owners) were killed, and Indian, mestizo, and Creole troops had learned the dangerous glory of war, loot, uniforms, and medals. Liberals and conservatives were at odds.

In 1821 the shrewd, handsome, and ambitious young Col. Agustín de Iturbide proclaimed the Plan of Iguala with its three main objectives: independence from Spain; equal treatment for Spaniards and Creoles (no mention of lesser breeds); the supremacy of the Catholic religion. His army, known as the *Trigarante*, would enforce this triple program. How could he miss? The plan pleased everyone but the Indians and mestizos, who didn't count as political forces.

On September 27, 1821, three centuries after the Conquest, Mexico was "free" and, briefly, united. Iturbide set up claques of enthusiasts in Mexico City for his triumphant entry and eight months later permitted himself to be made Emperor. But he made the grave mistake of snubbing another ambitious and shrewd young officer, Antonio López de Santa Anna. The empire collapsed. When the exiled Emperor rashly returned in 1824, he was shot by a former friend.

Hidalgo and Allende, Morelos and Iturbide, Santa Anna —later Juárez, Maximilian, and Porfirio Díaz—these were the names to conjure with in the nineteenth century. For the next thirty years the rascally Santa Anna dominated the stage and led Mexico a merry chase from farce to tragedy.

Between 1833 and 1855 he skipped in and out of the presidency at his whim, retiring now and then to his ranch and fighting cocks. He won and lost battles, commanded the slaughter at the Alamo, lost the battle of San Jacinto during a siesta, and was captured by Sam Houston. He ceded Texas to the United States and returned to his country the next year—but the Mexican congress was so disobliging as to reject the cession.

During his sorry administrations Mexico lost Texas, Arizona, New Mexico, and California. The government was so rotten with corruption that respectable people withdrew from public life. Militarism became rampant. At one time the army consisted of 20,000 troops and 24,000 officers! When Santa Anna lost his leg in battle, he had the grotesque pleasure of having it interred and later exhumed and brought in state to the capital to be buried anew with all military honors!

In 1846 the Mexican-American War occurred, in which a young lieutenant named Ulysses S. Grant took part. He later described it as "one of the most unjust ever waged by a stronger against a weaker nation. . . . We were sent to provoke a fight, but it was essential that Mexico should commence it." It was in this shameful war that the United States invaded Mexico, captured the capital (because the jealous Santa Anna refused to share battle honors with another general and withdrew his forces from the field!), and forced the Treaty of Guadalupe Hidalgo, which ceded half the territory of Mexico to the United States for $15,000,000—in defiance of our own Monroe Doctrine. This war gave Mexico its *Niños Héroes*, the young cadets who defended the military citadel of Chapultepec to the last, as a focus for its bitter memory of the invaders. Santa Anna's army dissolved, and he sought refuge in Oaxaca from its governor, a Zapotec Indian named Benito Juárez (a name to be remembered). Juárez refused him, so Santa Anna surrendered, entertained his captors at a banquet, and sailed away into exile. It was temporary, of course.

The cities and states of Mexico were virtually independent. The country's treasury was empty, its morality bankrupt, its morale at low ebb. The mestizos and Indians had fought the Revolution of 1810 and gone wild with loot, rape, and massacre, but it was the Creole who landed on top at the end. It was only after the Indian Juárez came into power that the mestizos began to acquire military and political influence by the weight of numbers and by flurries of political talent. Mexico City held sway over the central regions of Mexico, but the vast territories remote from this center were difficult to control. They felt little identification with the government, and the political dissolution that eventually severed the bonds merely made the break official. It was the reverse of our own history, which began with a small slice of territory on the Eastern Seaboard and gradually pressed westward as the population, power, and needs of the nation grew by purchase, war, or treaty.

In 1853 Santa Anna was recalled, for the last time, as a dictator. Resourcefully he sold part of Arizona to the United States for $10,000,000 to buy more fancy uniforms, coaches, and the loyalty of his generals for a little longer. Then in 1855 he went again into exile. (It is to Santa Anna that we owe that devastating item, chewing gum. During this exile in the United States, his American secretary James Adams noticed the General's habit of chewing chicle, sap from the trees of Yucatán. And that developed into a billion-dollar industry.)

Juárez entered the national scene in 1855 and dominated it until his death in 1872. An Indian from the hills, he had worked as a houseboy in the city of Oaxaca. He so impressed his patron that he was given an education, first for the priesthood and later for the law, which was more to his taste.

It was Juárez who masterminded the separation of church and state—such a drastic step in a Catholic country—the expropriation of church properties worth 200,000,-000 pesos, the proclamation of religious liberty and civil marriage, the suppression of monasteries and nunneries, and the prohibition of religious habits of dress. These and other principles, including state direction of education, were embodied in the liberal constitution of 1857 and in the reform laws that followed two years later.

What were intended as liberal measures had some catastrophic effects. Properties in the hands of the church had been well managed and productive, and education under church jurisdiction had been on a comparatively high level. After the reform laws went into effect, the country lost ground economically and educationally, and it was sharply split again between liberals and conservatives.

The chaos of Mexico was an invitation to foreign intercession. Napoleon III in France allied himself with the Church and Mexican conservatives (and briefly with England and Spain). On the pretext of collecting debts and pacifying the country, he sent 34,000 troops, arranged a plebescite, and placed his puppet, the Austrian Archduke Maximilian, on the imperial throne of Mexico.

It was not to be the picnic that Napoleon III anticipated. In the victory over the French at Puebla on May 5, 1862, the Mexicans gave notice that they could be fierce fighters by any standards. The country was torn between the conservatives, aided by the Church and foreign powers, and the liberals represented by Juárez and his government in exile.

Maximilian arrived in 1864 with his handsome wife Car-

lotta, a detailed set of court rituals, vague liberal aspirations, and excellent intentions. He hopefully invited Juárez
to a meeting to achieve a reconciliation. But Juárez was
adamant. In his view Maximilian was leading a criminal as-
sault upon the established government of a nation, and
Juárez proposed to wage war against the invader until the
justice of his cause was accepted.

The foreign invasion intensified the amorphous sense
of nationalism and welded the country into something like
a nation. Maximilian alienated conservatives by wooing
the liberals, and both the Pope and the French Emperor
failed him. Carlotta left on a futile mission to persuade
them to keep their solemn promises and went mad in the
Vatican. In Mexico, Maximilian listened to unscrupulous
advisers, vacillated, and made worse mistakes until he himself recognized the hopelessness of his reign and was prepared to abdicate.

At the last minute he changed his mind. He joined his
dwindling army at Querétaro with Generals Miramón and
Mejía. He suffered the anguish of the siege, watched the
bodies of his supporters float down the river into town,
and ignored a chance to escape when his army broke
through the liberal forces. He was captured at last, betrayed by one of his favored officers.

Always personally loved and admired by his retinue and
followers, in his death Maximilian became a hero. He was
shot on the Hill of the Bells at Querétaro in 1867, and his
body was returned to Europe on the same ship that had
brought him in state to Mexico.

Stern Juárez rode into Mexico City in his black coach,
and he in his turn antagonized an admirer, the young Porfirio Díaz. Maximilian lives in memory as a martyred prince

and beautifier of the capital. Juárez survives as a myth and an abstraction, austere and cold, a man of integrity. Yet he resorted to fraud in elections because he felt it was the only way to carry out the constitution, which had established universal male suffrage in a country 90 per cent illiterate. In Juárez for the first time the Indian blood of the nation gained power and recognition. Unfortunately, he also established the tradition that a government candidate should win any election by devious means against opposing candidates.

Four years after the death of Juárez, the young mestizo Porfirio Díaz overthrew Sebastián Lerdo de Tejada, his successor, and ruled with hardly a break from 1876 to 1911. For nearly thirty-five years he was the prime example of a benevolent despot. The wealthy adored him for his efficiency on their behalf—and his. He made the country safe for travelers and tourists, established reliable train service, and initiated free schools. He favored foreign investments, governed astutely, and presented Mexico with a fine façade of civilization. Order and progress became his slogan. He crushed banditry and militarism, encouraged the growth of industry, built five thousand more schools, and gave the national treasury a surplus instead of a deficit. Each town had its plaza and bandstand. Mexicans abroad could be proud of their country's status. There is still a lingering admiration for Don Porfirio and his accomplishments—but not among the neglected Indians and mestizos.

Desirable though these accomplishments were, they represented only a thin veneer of civilization, an aping of European and especially French culture. The campesinos were worse off then ever. During the Díaz regime the hacienda system thrived. A thousand families owned the greater part of Mexico, and a single estate in Chihuahua was the size of Belgium, Holland, Switzerland, and Denmark put together—over 26,000,000 acres. Naturally the hacendados were admirers of Díaz.

The Indians and mestizos were not. Even their ejidos, lands worked in common by the farmers, were appropriated and redistributed to friends and followers of the dictator. Hundreds of thousands of peons worked on haciendas in virtual bondage. They were underpaid, underfed, and poorly sheltered, constantly held by debts, unable to better themselves by leaving for other work. So the gulf between high and low, between twentieth-century urbanites and twelfth-century Indian serfs, grew deeper, wider, and more dangerous.

On the surface Díaz looked indestructible. His tacit alliance with the Church, which was permitted gradual resumptions of powers and riches, enhanced his prestige. Since his marriage to the pious and beautiful young Doña Carmen Rubio, he had grown respectable. He had learned proper table manners and unpretentious dress, and his mestizo skin even seemed to lighten. But Mexico was tiring of the decades of dictatorship and grew restive when there was no hint of a successor to the septuagenarian Díaz.

In an interview with an American journalist, who came full of admiration for him as the greatest man in the hemisphere, Díaz tossed out a verbal bomb. He felt, he said, that Mexico with its thriving middle class was now ready for a democracy and an opposition party, and he intended to retire in 1910.

A young hacendado and parlor liberal, little Francisco

Madero, naïvely took him at his word. He campaigned for president, lost in 1910, and was clapped into jail. He escaped to the United States and sounded a call to revolution. This went unheeded until he met the bandit-general Pancho Villa. Their meeting set off the Revolution (with a capital R) that raged for ten bloody years.

Like the Russian Revolution of 1917, it was sporadic and occurred in many areas as a result of the craving for land, liberty, justice, and bread. Unlike the Russian Revolution, it was never focused on one ideology, nor was it dominated by two or three powerful leaders. Instead it was and remained a rather formless but violent expression of revenge and vague ambitions with a host of leaders at odds among themselves.

Emiliano Zapata of the south joined with Villa of the north to enter the capital in triumph on behalf of Madero. The early morning of President Madero's appearance on the scene in 1911 was marked by an earthquake all too symbolic of catastrophe. Fifteen months later Madero was betrayed and shot under circumstances that hinted at unwarranted intervention by the United States Ambassador. The Revolution continued, and by 1920 the old order was finally overturned. Gen. Alvaro Obregón became President. By then, a million Mexicans had died in battle, or of disease or starvation, and the country was heartily sick of bloodshed and destruction.

The Constitution of 1917 of Querétaro had reconstructed that of 1857 and added some new frills. Article 3 made public education secular and primary education compulsory (but not *very* compulsory because there weren't enough schools, teachers, or means of enforcement). Article 27 reclaimed land owned by foreigners and asserted the right of popular sovereignty over it so that it reverted to the nation. Article 123 in one stroke attempted the leap from feudalism to the industrial age. It recognized the right of labor to organize, strike, bargain collectively, and receive suitable pay and sick benefits. There was also severe limitation of the number of priests, plus confiscation of church lands.

Obregón tried to make the new constitution more than a blueprint and was most successful in regard to education. This secretariat was headed by José Vasconcelos, a prime example of the capable scholar-philosopher-statesman. The labor program speedily became a cynical grab for power and money by its leaders, whose taste for graft and force filtered down into the ranks. Since according to the constitution no president could succeed himself, Obregón named as his successor Plutarco Elías Calles.

Calles was another despot, but he continued educational efforts, road building and maintenance, and some redistribution of land back to the peasants. He was rigorously anticlerical, closed all religious schools, and deported nuns and priests. The clergy struck back, and the Cristero rebellion began with the burning of government schools and the killing of government teachers. The Calles men retaliated unmercifully.

Obregón was assassinated, and Calles remained the strong man of Mexico through a series of puppet presidents. At last his own candidate, Gen. Lázaro Cárdenas, quietly built up a following after election, surprised his sponsor by a showdown, and exiled him to the United States. Cárdenas was the first chief executive to campaign among the people, the first with a genuine regard for the welfare of the peasant. He was beloved for being approachable and for listening to the personal complaints and problems of citizens. He distributed more acreage to the peons, started a credit bank to finance agriculture, opened the country to refugees from the Spanish civil war, built roads, dams, schools, irrigation projects, and promoted communal ejidos in the old tradition to replace the little *milpas*, cornpatches farmed by individuals.

On March 18, 1938, he defied foreign investment interests and their governments by expropriating oil properties. But Utopia was not achieved on that day. The nationalized oil and railroad industries were shockingly mismanaged. Yet the action served notice on the world that Mexico had status and self-respect, and it increased the citizens' growing sense of nationalism.

With Calles the Revolutionary Party (known now as PRI, the *Partido Revolucionario Institucional*) became *the* political power of the country. Presidents must live with this fact of life and must work amicably with the elements represented in it—state political bosses, labor unions, peasant organizations, and the army.

The President of Mexico is elected by popular vote for a six-year term and cannot be re-elected. He governs with a Cabinet of fourteen Ministers and a two-house federal Congress—the Senate and the Chamber of Deputies. These members have limited power. They neither voice public opinion nor serve as critics of executive policy to the extent that our congressmen do.

Presidential powers are greater than in our country. The president initiates most legislation. He names and removes high officials, including diplomatic agents, with little interference. He may even replace state administrations of which he disapproves. In effect, the President *is* the government of Mexico, but he has to cope with or submit to strong influences by previous presidents and work closely with the PRI.

There are twenty-nine states, plus two federal territories and a federal district whose governors are appointed by the President. The states have a large measure of autonomy, but the state elections of governors and lesser municipal officers are virtually dictated by the President and the PRI.

There is a Supreme Court of twenty-one members named by the President and ratified by the Senate. Thus there are the three divisions of executive, legislative, and judicial, which in theory exercise a check upon each other. Married males can vote at eighteen and single men at twenty-one. Since 1953, women have had suffrage and can vote at the same age as men.

The one-party government, the PRI, is modestly challenged by a conservative party. With few exceptions the PRI has determined all "elections." Recent efforts to liberalize its methods by presenting alternate candidates on occasion and allowing nominations from the floor at conventions for local offices have sometimes been checked. The great strength of the PRI is that it really represents the nation. Its members compose a perfect rainbow of political beliefs, which makes it sensitive and responsive to the national will. It has shifted from the left under Cárdenas, to the right under Miguel Alemán, and back to the middle in the present administration under López Mateos. It has enabled Mexico to maintain for two decades a political stability unmatched in Latin America. Free speech and a free press are realities. Democracy gradually gains strength as the people grow more literate and politically educated and make their voice increasingly heard.

One of the most serious difficulties of government, and in fact of all phases of Mexican life, is graft in the form of the *mordida*. This is the "bite" that many persons feel entitled to take out of the simplest transaction. As in most Latin American countries, graft is a method of survival in a nation where rates of remuneration for a great part of the populace are unbelievably low.

Visitors from the United States are most conscious of the mordida at the border, where customs officials sometimes encourage gratuities. But this has been changing since the reform administration of President Adolfo Ruiz Cortines (1952-1958), and the government often cracks down hard on some of the most outrageous forms of graft. Now travelers are sometimes faced with an inflexible official when they try a small bribe. As for unions, one disgusted member, according to Oscar Lewis in *Five Families*, says, "The union leaders grab the secretary general and get together their gang of four or five men and say, 'The company is ready to pay the wages we want, right? Let's tell them to give less and we'll take 50 per cent of the raise and give the workers 20 per cent!' "

With a gradual rise in the standard of living, a wider recognition of the value of integrity in both national and personal life, and the examples of more public figures of probity, there is hope that graft will diminish as an accepted practice.

The Mexican government is neither socialist nor capitalist but a special mixture of its own. Electric power, the National Railways of Mexico, the oil industry, and some four hundred others of greater or less importance are run by the government, and not with maximum economy. But the government takes the view that it must accomplish in crucial areas what private enterprise is unwilling or unable to do because of the financial risks or losses involved. Hence it undertakes many projects that are anything but profitable, because in the long run they will prove valuable to the national economy and welfare. These include huge projects of dams, irrigation, and road building.

The government tries to subsidize or aid the campesinos through credit banks—but much of the money fills the pockets of well-organized big ranchers who need it far less than the peons. One of the problems of administering foreign aid is that loans are made on terms that seem to be usury, typical of an underprivileged country where cash is terribly hard to get. The interest terms often run to 18 and 20 per cent and more. However, recent experiments with small loans at low rates of interest have been remarkably successful.

Immense progress has been made since the Revolution in a sustained program to bring a better life to the lower classes. There is a steady campaign to improve education, diet, habits of cleanliness, clothing, shelter, and health. Doctors are so scarce in Mexico (about 1 per 900 in the cities and 1 per 18,000 in rural areas) that since 1936 graduate medical students have been required to serve five months in a doctorless community. When a graduate chooses his post, he is given a place to live, office facilities, a small salary, and in return is expected to carry on health education and medical practice and make a report on the community. There are rural medical teams for primitive areas—doctor, nurse, midwife, pharmacist, and sanitary officer. More elaborate services have to be paid for partly by the community. A conspicuously successful effort at cooperation between public health services of Mexico and the United States provides mixed personnel from the two countries for medical assistance, health centers, sanitary engineering, and similar projects.

"Land and liberty!" has been the peon's cry for generations, but he needs much else besides. Too often he lives the same toilsome unrewarding life as his ancestors, in the same windowless, airless, dirt-floored, barren hut, working with the same primitive tools, battling almost hopelessly against the elements.

But the emphasis has necessarily been on tangible improvements rather than on the program of spiritual and civic betterment that was among the principal objectives of the Revolution.

5

At Home in Mexico

Home for a lucky city family may be a sleek contemporary house of lava rock in the Pedregal, a suburb of Mexico City built over lava beds, or a tiled, marbled, and many-arched mansion in Lomas, an older suburb. It may be a colonial house in the lovely old section of San Angel, another suburb, with its cobblestoned streets and magnificent trees. They differ from their counterparts in the United States in a more lavish use of tile, terrazzo and stone, and in their riotously blooming gardens of tropical trees and flowers—poinsettias, camellias, palms, bananas, frangipani, and jacaranda. The children may play in a fountain or shallow pool. Every house is walled or fenced in for privacy, but no one is a copy of its neighbor.

Or *home* may mean the handsome city apartment of a government employee, a bank official, a store owner, or a professor (with an independent income). The apartment resembles one in the United States except that the architecture may be more adventurous. Usually there is an inside wall of brick or stone, interior plants that grow immense,—and often the building needs repairs. There is seldom a trace of the Mexican crafts so prized by American tourists—basketry, ceramics, glassware, weaving—except in the home of an artist, writer, architect, archeologist, or other professional person. But there will be plenty

88

of electrical appliances. Central heating is rare and air conditioning almost unheard of. In Mexico City fireplaces or gas heaters supply what heat is needed, and the fresh cool air of the high altitude makes air conditioning unnecessary.

Home to an affluent resident of Guadalajara may be a copy of a French palace on a tree-lined street. In smaller cities like Salamanca, there are often settlements of neat little workers' houses.

Certain working-class families of large cities are well housed in apartments of striking architecture. They have playgrounds for children, murals by noted artists, swimming pools, nursery schools, and supermarkets. The Benito Juárez apartments of Mexico City, with one to four bedrooms and modest rents, are intended for government employees. The painted murals and sculpture are by Carlos Mérida. The development occupies 230,000 square meters of parkland of which only 13,000 are used for buildings, thus ensuring ample light, landscaping, and play areas. The Balbuena Gardens in a suburb of Mexico City will house 50,000 people in apartment units, row houses, and detached houses. There will be schools up to the college level, medical services, churches, and shopping and recreation centers. Three fourths of the area will be in parks and lawns.

But the story for nearly 2,000,000 inhabitants of Mexico City and other large cities is grim. They live in adobe huts; in shacks contrived from scraps of tin, wood, aluminum, and tile; in railroad cars at the edge of town; in rundown apartments and tenements and broken-down colonial buildings in the commercial districts. Often they live without adequate water, sanitary facilities, or space.

Their homes are comparable to the shacks of poor whites or Negroes in the southeastern United States or to much of the housing in our city slums—but worse. Many of these are known as *vecindades* (neighborhoods).

These house some of the unhappiest people in Mexico —those in transition. These are families caught in the movement from town to city, from barefoot peonage to the middle or working class, from illiteracy to garbled knowledge, from the traditional "wantlessness" of the Mexicans to the insatiable materialism of United States-influenced culture. Such are the people described in Oscar Lewis's *Five Families, Mexican Case Studies in the Culture of Poverty.* These families are marked by dreariness, deteriorating religious practices, broken marriages, desertion, and loss of the strong attachments and affectionate warmth so pronounced in most Mexican families. They lack the satisfaction of feeling themselves a coherent part of tradition, and they lack the rewards of emergence into a new stratum of society.

The mother becomes more dominant and often works outside the home. The children are harder to control. Installment buying and a desire for a better standard of living are noticeable. There is more leisure and there are broader contacts with other classes. Some of the old superstitions drop away; there is more dependence on doctors and medicine.

Most of these people have radios. More than half have gas stoves and watches. About half use knives and forks as well as spoons, have sewing machines, and aluminum rather than clay pots. Some have electric blenders, television sets, and washing machines, and about 5 per cent have cars and refrigerators. Eight per cent are illiterate.

According to the 1950 census of Mexico, of 5,200,000 houses 60 per cent had only one room, 25 per cent had two rooms; 70 per cent were made of wood, poles, adobe, rods, or rubble; 18 per cent were of brick and masonry, and only 17 per cent had piped water. But of houses built in 1962 in the Federal District, 7,000 were of concrete, about 200 of brick, and 8 of lumber. Adobe is disappearing from the urban picture. Today, 16 per cent of Mexicans own cars, 83 per cent own radios, and 24 per cent television sets.

The cities are beautified with fountains, flowers, modern markets, fine boulevards, but too many citizens still live in slums. People who could afford better housing often cannot find it, and they fill their tiny rooms with new furniture and appliances until they can scarcely move.

Near the Thieves' Market in Mexico City is a one-story tenement spread over an entire block, which houses more than seven hundred people. It is surrounded by walls on two sides and shops facing the streets on the other sides. Once it was an underworld hangout, but now it is the home of tradesmen, artisans, vendors, washwomen, chauffeurs, and factory workers. Its two entrances are locked at night, and anyone who uses the gates later must pay the janitor. The Virgin of Guadalupe and the Virgin of Zapopán each guard one entrance as patron saints.

Four long cement buildings inside are divided into 157 one-room apartments, each with a red door opening onto a patio. Crude ladders beside the doors lead to flat roofs over the kitchen sheds. These carry clotheslines, chicken coops and dovecotes, gas tanks, pots of flowers and herbs

—and sometimes TV antennae. By day the patios are crowded with small children, women hanging clothes or queueing up for water, with street vendors, the garbage man, and with dogs, pigs, and poultry. In the afternoon older children play soccer in one patio. On Sunday evenings there is usually an outdoor dance with a record player to supply music, and the young people dance to American, Cuban, and Mexican records until early morning. Near one entrance is a small garden with a few trees and a patch of grass where young people rendezvous and oldsters talk and read newspapers.

Except for the flowers and a generally neighborly attitude, the tenement looks dismal, but the inhabitants are proud of it and have a strong community sense. They organize raffles and mutual savings plans, celebrate Christmas posadas, festivals of the patron saints, and make religious pilgrimages together. The children attend the same schools, later meet at the dances, and often grow up to marry neighbors. Yet there is little visiting except among special friends or relatives; they maintain some privacy.

Still poorer is a vecindad on an open lot, a row of twelve tiny windowless one-room apartments housing fifty-four people. These too have a lean-to extending from the cement roofs to form a kitchen. At the rear is a cement water trough for laundry, dishes, and bathing children. Two toilets are curtained off by burlap for the use of all tenants. Even this dirt lot boasts flowerpots and singing birds in cages.

Here lives Guillermo with his family, his common-law wife Julia, and three children, aged nine to fourteen, by his former wife. Oscar Lewis in his book, *Five Families*, describes the optimistic Guillermo, the son of a teacher, as a kind of Mexican Mr. Micawber, a resourceful chap with more imagination than moral fiber. He once worked in a bicycle agency and after that held several jobs at one time. He delivered newspapers, worked in a bicycle factory, delivered mail and telegrams, made toys, repaired bicycles, and served as night watchman. When he worked in a paper factory and learned something about union rules, he began to devise tricks for getting sick benefits from the union. Rubbing garlic under his arms and soaking his feet in boiling water would produce a fever and an order to rest for three days. Intrigued by learning that a surgical operation meant 900 pesos for the afflicted worker, Guillermo ate twenty popsicles, got a sore throat, had a tonsillectomy, and received his 900 pesos. Next he tried to promote a hernia. Instead he succeeded in getting appendicitis—but another 900 pesos. Now he works at home, making toys and repairing bicycles.

Julia is a capable, cheerful older woman who often makes money by selling towels and other items on the streets. The commercial sections are best, but she avoids them so she won't have to bribe the police on the beat. Guillermo subscribes to the Information Bulletin of the U.S.S.R. because it provides him with free wrapping paper for his toys and pictures to look at when there is nothing else to do.

In their eight-foot-square inner room, only a narrow aisle is left for passage. A tiny half-balcony four feet wide juts out from one side a few feet above the floor and holds bedspring and mattress for the children, also bicycle rims, used tires, scrap iron, pots, and provisions. Under the balcony are old bicycles and boxes of empty soda bottles, a barrel of bicycle parts, and stacks of clothes.

Against the rear wall are a couple of chairs, the parents' bed, and a combination radio, record player, and television set protected by the original paper carton. Guillermo, the entrepreneur, pays for it by installments, expects it to earn one or two pesos a day from children who come to watch programs, and when it is paid for, he hopes to sell it as new.

It is customary on weekend evenings to pay a few centavos to the lucky neighbor who owns a TV set and to spend hours watching it. People stay up much later than they used to and no longer listen to the radio as much or attend movies so often. Children spend more time indoors. Girls dress more fashionably and people buy more on the installment plan as a result of advertising on TV. People acquire new ideas—one child wants to become a ballet dancer after seeing a dance group on TV.

Fortunately, not all families fall into the category of those reported in *Five Families*. An example of the new generation of career girls is tall, pretty Teresa Narezo. When she was small, her Spanish father died, and her mother took her and an older sister to live for a few years in the United States. Her school years in New Jersey and California gave her the foundation for a good knowledge of English. In Mexico she studied Spanish shorthand for two years and later took a month of English shorthand.

At sixteen she began working as a bilingual secretary. Her first job was with an insurance company, her second with an advertising agency. Since she had always wanted to travel, she took examinations to become a secretary in the diplomatic corps. She passed with honors and was assigned as secretary to the Mexican Ambassador to West Germany at Cologne. Once abroad, she became interested

in a diplomatic career and more conscious of the responsibility of knowing more about her country so that she could
explain it to foreigners.

Now she has been appointed press attachée. She reads
the papers and transcribes what is interesting to Mexico,
talks with colleagues to learn their points of view and to
convey the Mexican viewpoint, and attends diplomatic
and economic functions. On vacations she travels all over
Europe and Britain. Recently she has taken examinations
for vice-consul, though she is only twenty-three. She
wants to make a career in foreign service and employ
her knowledge of Spanish, English, and German.

Life for city people has more parallels with ours at all
levels, but only about one-fourth of the population of
35,000,000 in Mexico lives in cities of more than 100,000.
More than 5,000,000 of these live in Mexico City itself,
the sixth-largest city in the world. A higher percentage of
city people are literate, and their children attend school
more regularly. They dress more or less like us and often
with extreme chic. They ride crowded buses to work
(for three cents a ride or less) or can hail a peso cab that
travels the length of a main avenue, like Insurgentes or the
Paseo de la Reforma, and drops the passenger anywhere
on that route for eight cents, or take a regular cab for
two or three pesos.

Shops have metal shutters for protection at night, and
these are rolled back for the day at 10 A.M. Mexico City's
shops stay open weekdays, without a siesta period, until
6 P.M. They are closed on Sundays. In smaller cities shops
close for two or three hours of lunch and siesta in the
afternoon and stay open until 8 P.M., with one day off

during the week instead of Sunday, which is often market day.

But many of the country people lead the life of two or three centuries ago. They may still use iron hand plows, plant by hand, reap by hand, and load the produce on a burro or two-wheeled cart for the market or even carry it on their own head and shoulders.

The Martínez family, described in *Five Families*, lives in a small highland village in a one-room, windowless adobe hut with slanted tiled roof. Its adjoining tiny kitchen shelter has two walls of cane stalks. A metal bed for the father and mother, Pedro and Esperanza, stands there, screened off by crates, and in another corner their daughter and grandson sleep. Their older daughter is married and has her own home.

The inner room is the bedroom for the four sons and also contains a chest full of books and clothing, stools, chairs, and benches, and a wooden table covered with religious pamphlets, Bibles, school texts, comic books, and novels. In the yard are plants and trees—coffee, avocado, hog plums.

The older daughter Conchita attended the state normal school for three years while her father worked as a peon to earn her expenses, hoping to be recompensed by her prestige and earnings as a teacher. Unfortunately, she came home pregnant, which infuriated her father. After the birth of the baby, she went away again to teach and sent home gifts—a mirror, a silk dress, shoes, a flashlight, etc.—for the younger children, her mother, and her son —and thirty pesos a month. She later married a village lad, but the marriage was a tumultuous one and left bad feelings.

Seventeen-year-old Machrina wanted to become a teacher or seamstress but was taken out of school to help her mother. The boys leave with their father in the morning to work some of the communal land of the village. To make new fields, they burn brush and weeds, cut down young trees, build new stone fences. They grow enough corn and beans for three or four months at a time. They also make rope from maguey fiber, sell plums, and work as farmhands for private property owners. All speak Nahuatl and Spanish. The family earns about $300 a year and is constantly in debt and verging on starvation.

Pedro had been an ardent Catholic but was converted to a Protestant sect and ostracized by the villagers who had before regarded him highly. Despite social disapproval, it was a happier time for the family because Pedro stopped drinking and gave up his political activities to concentrate on earnings and his family. Recently he has been disillusioned by leaders of his new religion and is drifting back toward Catholicism.

The typical middle-class family of a smaller city lives in a building that surrounds a patio bright with flowers, trees, and a fountain or shallow pool for conserving water. The rooms have lofty ceilings with exposed rafters supporting bricks, and most have fireplaces. Those facing the street have tall, iron-grated windows. Others simply have doorways leading to the patio or another room. Unless they have glass apertures in the ceiling, all light comes from the open doors, so however gay the patio, interior rooms are often dark and gloomy.

The *sala* is furnished with a massive sofa and chairs, a coffee table, china knickknacks on shelves, and artificial flowers rather than the real blooms so close at hand. The floor is tiled or of terrazzo or rubbed brick. In the better homes there are bookshelves, perhaps with biographies, histories, encyclopedias, and Spanish editions of novels by Pearl Buck, Dostoevsky, or Zola, and Mexican novels. Electric wires run exposed along the walls, but there is small danger of fire with the absence of wood, the high altitude, and the thick stone walls.

A shining new refrigerator often stands in the dining room. Bedrooms are simply furnished—beds, chests, a wardrobe (closets are rare), and a chair or two. Usually there is a large bathroom with modern plumbing and fixtures, but water must be heated by wood or gas in a *calentador*. In back there may be a stable or corral beyond the patio, and at the entrance you may stand aside while a *mozo* (servant) leads a saddled horse through the great wooden doors into the street.

The total effect is one of dignity and space, and the patio lends brilliance with its color, the singing of bright yellow or crimson birds, or the squawking and scolding of a green-plumaged parrot.

A similar building next door may house several poor families living together but usually without benefit of plumbing. Single electric bulbs dangle nakedly from the ceiling of some rooms. Furniture is at a minimum, and the beds are no more than straw mats that can be stretched on the ground at night. Pigs roam around the patio with a couple of burros or goats for company. Babies crawl naked in the sun or sit quietly in the arms of a mother or sister, watching from unblinking black eyes. The year round, the walls are massed with color from bougainvillea, geraniums, lilies, and poinsettias.

The independent townsman is likely to be a jack-of-all-trades and have his fingers in several pies. A blacksmith may own a cab or truck and some real estate which he rents. Many men are mozos, handymen who work for Mexican or foreign families.

Juan Rojas is a husky man of thirty who was brought up by his mother and stepfather. He left school at the age of eleven after little more than two years, when his stepfather fell sick and Juan had to earn money for the family. First he worked in a home for a peso and a meal a day and occasionally some clothing, from early morning to late at night. His next job, from only seven in the morning to seven at night at a rate of two pesos a day, was like play to him. After several other jobs, one lasting for two years, another for seven, with steady raises in pay, he works now for a foreign family from seven-thirty in the morning to six in the evening. He finds the variety of his work and the somewhat higher salary stimulating. He can repair plumbing, install a new electric line, garden, groom horses, tend stables and horses, clean and repair riding gear, or serve at bar and buffet.

He lives in a brick house that he and his family built in a pleasant section of town. They have running water and hope to install electricity next year. There is a main entrance into two sizable rooms, with a large and a small kitchen in the back (the small one is exclusively for making tortillas by wood fire, which gives a better taste), and this year he has completed a bathroom. He shares this house with his wife and six children, his father and mother, married brothers and sisters—a total of fourteen. Yet when a pilgrimage came through town in the winter and an unseasonable deluge left the pilgrims without shelter, his family fed fifty of them and housed some fifteen or twenty for the night. For all Juan's hard work and cares, he is a man of great energy, boundless good humor, and devout religious sense.

On a main street of San Miguel de Allende hangs a sign, *Carmela, Salon de Belleza* (Beauty Shop). Carmen Aguado is a very pretty brown-eyed girl of twenty who attended primary school in the city and then spent a year as apprentice to a beauty operator in a neighboring town. At sixteen, with some help from her parents, she established her own shop with a minimum of equipment in the back of a store. Now she has the whole shop, her own apprentices, all in uniform, with up-to-date equipment— and a stack of magazines in English and Spanish. She has also opened next door a shop of hand-embroidered clothing for children. She often works from seven in the morning till midnight, especially when local balls and beauty contests are impending.

Strangers in San Miguel are sometimes surprised to pass a storefront embellished with the Star of David. Forty years ago the elder Cohen came to Mexico from Damascus and traveled through the country as a merchant. Five years later he settled in San Miguel and established a fabric shop, which gradually was expanded to include almost anything from eggbeaters and garbage pails to lumber and bedroom furniture. Ten children were born, and when the father died, young David Cohen gave up his study of engineering in Mexico City to become head of the family and the business. A zestful, busy young man, he likes dancing, bowling, and a fast game of *fronton* (jai alai) but is so occupied with business and civic matters (he has been president of the Lions Club and the Chamber of Commerce and a member of the governing body of the city) that there is little time for recreation. He and his family continue in the Jewish faith by attending a synagogue in Mexico City and going to the capital for the major holidays.

At another extreme are the people of certain isolated Indian communities—the primitive Lacandones of Chiapas, for example. These descendants of the Maya live in the jungles on mountainsides in small groups. One group lives in a village of eight huts, four open on all sides, four closed with vertical slats of wood. One hut contains sacred arrows, "god pots" that hold incense and have faces of the deities molded and painted on them, and other religious paraphernalia and is the scene of religious ceremonies. The people sleep on low platforms of wood that can be curtained off and take their siestas in hammocks. In garden patches near the village they grow corn, sweet potatoes, cassava, sugar cane, papayas, lemons, tomatoes, beans, tobacco, cotton, and other plants. They hunt deer, birds, mountain lions, tapirs, and other animals for food. Every three or four years they must break new land for farming. They do their work a few weeks before the rainy season, which in their land is most of the year except March and April.

They are a low-voiced, quiet people, apparently doomed to extinction. They laugh easily but are a reserved and somewhat melancholy tribe, suspicious of white men and their diseases. A few know a little Spanish, but most speak a dialect that differs little from the language of the ancient Maya. Men and women wear their hair long and dress in a tentlike garment, sometimes adorned with a scarf or necklace. They still burn the incense of sacred resin known as copal, worship some of the Maya gods, and drink the sacred intoxicant brewed from the sap of a tree. Occasionally, though they know little or nothing of their great ancestors and bear no trace of the skills, arts, and knowledge of mathematical and astronomical sciences for which the Maya are known, they make pilgrimages to their ancient ceremonial city, Palenque, forty miles away.

In poor homes a stove may be no more than three large stones or a *brasero*, a grill of iron or tin. Even in wealthy homes you may find a brasero next to the gas stove, though all other equipment is modern. Standard equipment in provincial kitchens requires a metate, a mortar and pestle for chiles and spices, clay bowls for cooking beans and stews, a pot for boiling meats, and a flat clay plate called a *comal* for cooking tortillas. All these were used for centuries before the Conquest. Although there are now mills for grinding corn, some women still prefer the old slow way of grinding it on a metate. Corn for tortillas is first soaked two or three days in limewater, then ground into a paste called *masa*. Tortillas are bread and entree, and they even serve as spoon or ladle.

More modern housewives pride themselves on owning aluminum or enamelware. The housewife with an electric blender is happy indeed and uses it constantly.

Mexican meals are served at different hours from ours. The campesino rises before daylight to drink coffee or *atole* (a thin gruel of maize). His wife wakes long before that to make tortillas. About eight he comes in from the fields for beans, tortillas, and coffee. In midafternoon he eats tortillas, beans, rice, or a bit of meat and soup, and perhaps small green chiles eaten raw with the beans. In the evening he has coffee or hot chocolate with tortillas or sweet rolls.

His urban cousin—in the middle or upper class—may have breakfast about eight, but his midday meal is a full-course dinner served at two or later. This means rolls, hot soup; *sopa seca* (dry soup, that is rice, macaroni, or spaghetti, sometimes with eggs); then fish, chicken, or game; salad; main course of meat and vegetables; fried beans with cheese; dessert of stewed fruit, pudding, or custard; then coffee and a plate of fresh fruit. Afterwards—no wonder—a siesta. In the evening, about eight or nine, comes a light supper.

This schedule is changing gradually in the large cities in favor of shorter lunches and a more leisurely late dinner.

Mexicans have always been prodigious consumers of soft drinks, which are made from lime, cantaloupe, watermelon, and even alfalfa. Now they are the world's champion customers for cola drinks. Milk has recently become popular and in some places is pasteurized. Hot chocolate originated with the Mexicans of old and is still a prime favorite. Nescafé is served everywhere, but Café Oro or Café Pronto or other instant brands, are sometimes available too. Soft drinks and excellent beer are popular beverages. The maguey yields several kinds of drink in various stages, beginning with honey water, which is drunk in some areas by old and young alike and supplies a good share of nutrition in the Mexican diet.

Among favorite dishes are tacos (tortillas fried in oil and wrapped around chicken, cheese, ground meat, or egg); enchiladas (stuffed tortillas served with a hot sauce); *frijoles refritos* (beans cooked and then refried into a paste); carnitas served in tortillas, sometimes with cut avocado; and good soups.

Don't look for chili con carne; it's a United States dish

rarely found in Mexico. Eggs *ranchero*, tamales (ground meat, well seasoned and wrapped in corn husks), roast kid, and *guacamole* (sauce made with avocado) are other popular dishes. Chicken and beef are usually tough, but other meats are usually tender and tasty.

Mole is a blend of a variety of chiles and spices made in different ways. Most famous is *mole poblana*, which has a complex recipe, requires two days of preparation, and is served mostly on holidays. Rice is an important part of the diet, along with beans and corn. Except in seaside villages and large cities, seafood is not popular. Mexican breads are excellent, crisp outside and soft within, and appear in a countless number of forms.

Fruits abound, but apples are expensive, and peaches, pears, and plums either small or rare. Most fruits we know are available and a great number that we do not know. A *limón* in Mexico is a lime and used as we use lemons. The larger *lima* is more like our lemon. There are pineapples, grapefruit, avocados, oranges, mangos, and all kinds of melons: watermelon, Persian, honeydew, and cantaloupe. Also there are *zapotes*, *camotes*, *tejocotes*, and a cactus fruit called *tuna*. *Jícamas* look like spherical turnips, but inside the grayish peel is a snowy, juicy meat that is delicious served in slices with a bit of salt and lime juice.

It is curious that although in the provinces restaurants are often mediocre, nearly everywhere in private homes the cooking is very tasty. Most Mexican cooks are masters at making soups.

There are still some quaint courting and marriage customs surviving from pre-Conquest days. Among the Tarascans it is customary to "steal" the bride (usually with

her consent) and take her to the house of a relative of the
groom, and the union is consummated while the wedding
is being arranged by relatives and a marriage maker.
Among the Seris of Sonora a man buys his bride with a
canoe or catch of fish or other goods, but he must also
please the whole family. There are sometimes mass wed-
dings in which the brides dress in regional costumes, for
example, in full skirt and *quexquemetl* (the triangular
shawl) and a square of cotton cloth on the head, and the
men wear white cotton suits adorned with red bandannas
for good luck.

Except in the strictest or most provincial of aristocratic
and even lower-class families, it is no longer typical of
courtship for the girl to see her *novio* (sweetheart) only
in the company of her family. There remains a high degree of supervision, but she is occasionally allowed a date
at the movies or a concert with her fiancé or a stroll in
the park on Sunday unescorted. In the towns one sees
courting couples holding hands in the street or in dark
doorways instead of through the window grating as before. The career girl of the cities is much more independent
and is granted much more freedom.

But one of the charming sights on Sunday evenings in
plazas all over Mexico is the promenade to the music of
the municipal band. Girls in their Sunday best parade in
twos and threes in one direction and the boys circle in
the opposite direction in a form of institutionalized flirta-
tion, which for years has been the approved beginning of
courtship. On special holidays the boys throw confetti
at the favored girls and crack eggshells filled with confetti over their chosen ones.

Once married, the young Mexican wife is dominated

as a rule by her husband. She is expected to run the household, raise children, visit friends at home, participate in charitable work, and do little else. Many a Mexican wife is left at home when her husband attends social functions. When husbands and wives do go to a party together, the sexes tend to separate. At one end of the room the women gossip or talk of children and household matters, while at the other end the men discuss business, sports, politics, literature, and philosophy. But a woman of character exercises influence everywhere, and in sophisticated Mexican circles social life is much like our own.

Marriages with foreigners are widely accepted now, but the Mexican husband is the boss of the family. He tends to be more suspicious and jealous than an American—and more solicitous too. He expects a much greater degree of attention than his northern counterpart. A Mexican wife seldom appears in public with a man who is not a member of the family. Families remain much closer after marriage, and it is usual to find a young couple accommodating a set of parents and unmarried brothers and sisters in their home.

Children are usually courteous and considerate of their parents. In the provinces they kiss the hand of a father returning from work or of a visitor or a priest. Children of wealthier parents can be fully as obnoxious as the most spoiled youngsters of the United States, but most tend to be quiet and well-behaved.

Like children everywhere, they dance and scream with excitement at fiestas on birthdays and holidays when they take turns at being blindfolded and thrashing with a stick at the festive *piñata* (a clay pot festooned with paper in the shape of a yellow rooster, black bull, white colt, or purple burro, filled with sweets, nuts, and tiny toys). The piñata is jerked up and down on cords until some child breaks the clay jar with his stick—then all the children dive on the floor to gather the treasures.

The traditional gift-giving to children occurs on January 6, the Day of the Three Kings, but with the advent of television and foreign influences, Christmas too is celebrated with presents and dinners and Christmas trees. Poor children have a marvelous facility for enjoying the smallest and most fractured toys—the head and torso of a limbless doll, a single skate, a broken bicycle, two miniature soldiers, or the pretty sugar creations sold on the Day of the Dead in the form of dolls, jaguars, sheep, burros, and anteaters.

Girls and women of the lower classes are remarkably independent and self-reliant. There are many desertions and separations, and a girl in her teens (many are married at fifteen or sixteen) may have to support herself and babies while the husband works elsewhere as a laborer, perhaps in the United States. He may come home months or a year later laden with presents or with bulging wallet, but meantime his wife has taken work as a maid, cook, or waitress. At work she keeps the baby with her in a box if she has not been able to leave it at home with a neighbor or relative or even an older child. This, of course, means unavoidable neglect, and far too many unattended babies and small children suffer fatal accidents or illnesses. It also means that the older children assume responsibilities very early. Sons remain very protective of mother and sisters.

One of the great blessings of Mexico for the middle and upper classes is the availability of domestic help. Even poor homes frequently hire maids (at $4 or $5 per week and up in the provinces, $5 or $6 and up in the cities). Some live in and are allowed a day off during the week. Others live at home, arrive in early morning, and leave at dusk or at night. In the cities they are protected by strict regulations, and the employer pays for medical care and other benefits. Even in the provinces it is usual to pay medical expenses. A conscientious employer often foots the bill for funerals in the family, extra schooling, and even jail fines. Most maids are not high-speed operators and require much supervision, but they are very faithful and especially good with children. A few are jewels of initiative and capability.

The market, the church, and the fiestas provide most of the social and spiritual sustenance of the lives of the poorer Mexicans. The market is a social occasion far beyond a commercial operation. If you meet a campesino on his way to market with bottles full of rough opals, he will cheerfully bargain with you. You may arrive at a satisfactory price for certain individual opals and even for the whole lot. But if you are then so tactless as to suggest buying all of them, the vendor is horrified. He will agree that you arrived at a fair price, but if he sold you his whole stock, there would be no reason for him to go to the market and the whole day would be spoiled. Politely he bids you good-by and goes on his way, pondering the lack of understanding of the gringos.

The fiestas are another form of release. The entire family journeys to town even if they must sleep at night on straw or palm-leaf mats called *petates*, on the street or under the arcades. Fiestas occur with frequency, and some attract celebrants from all over Mexico—like the Day of the Dead in Pátzcuaro, or carnival time in Veracruz.

Most beloved of all religious centers is the Shrine of Guadalupe outside of Mexico City. In December of 1531, after the destruction of the pagan deities and their shrines, legend has it that the Virgin appeared to a simple peasant, Juan Diego, on the spot where an Aztec goddess had been worshiped. She bade Juan tell the bishop that she wished a church to be erected on that hill. In token of the authenticity of his vision, Juan offered the bishop a capeful of roses he had gathered at the Virgin's bidding and on the cape miraculously appeared her image.

In 1754 a Papal Bull declared Our Lady of Guadalupe the Patroness and Protectress of New Spain. Revolutions have been fought under her standard—and when the enemy captured her banner, they shot at her image as though she were a traitor. On December 12, the anniversary of her appearance to Juan Diego, pilgrims gather from all of Mexico to walk the mile from the city to the shrine—sometimes on their knees. At dawn, songs and dances are performed in the church. Later at the top of the hill where three freshly made crosses are erected, the people dance around and offer incense to them and to the four cardinal points as they did in the time of the Aztecs. After worship, the pilgrims visit the nearby market, buy little corn cakes wrapped in colored paper, medallions of the Virgin, candles, and amulets. In a grand finale they have their pictures taken before exotic painted backdrops.

The church is a refuge and a delight, and all but the poorest of beggars will find some centavos to offer. The padre is father of his flock, and his word is law. Never mind that the peon must spend his hard-earned pesos for every church occasion, from a wedding (if he can afford one; about 20 per cent of the marriages in Mexico are free unions for lack of money for church or civil ceremony), to the birth and baptism of his children, their confirmation, their marriage and their death. The peon and his family enter the magnificent church feeling that some of this ivory, gold, and marble splendor is theirs and that the dark-skinned saints and the Virgin in her shrine, mistress of heaven and earth, are there to safeguard them.

The whole life of the peon is lived in a cycle—selling, buying, bartering in the market, fiestas or holidays, worship, pilgrimages and processions—and more work.

6

Crusade for Literacy

From the squeals and laughter, you might think you were approaching a school recess in the United States. But as you pass the gated entrance of a state school for girls and mount the steps, you note a few differences. There are more thin, undernourished children. A few have lack-luster eyes and too little energy to play. Some wear tattered or much-mended dresses. Others are spotlessly clean and fresh, and one tot wears blouse and toreador pants. They are brunettes, usually with braids neatly coiled, interwoven with red or yellow ribbons, or hanging in pigtails with bows. Some wear earrings.

The building, on grounds that are landscaped with tall pines, is a handsome two-story former residence. It is beautiful with balconies, ironwork, exquisite stonework decoration, and many windows. The rooms are mainly well lit and flooded with sunlight. Most schoolrooms lack heating facilities.

Because few children attend school beyond the primary grades, the curriculum is more concentrated than ours. The little girls of six or seven, in first grade, have been studying seven months; already they read clearly and without hesitation or stumbling over four- and five-syllable words. Most write as clearly as adults in a nice script; they line up proudly to display their neat notebooks.

A third-grade program might include: the geography of Mexico and the state; grammar, syllabification, the study of consonants, vowels, and diphthongs; a smattering of botany and anatomy; arithmetic (long division, fractions, and decimals); civics; little stories from history—and geometry!

By the end of six years the primary-school graduate is expected to know a good deal of Mexican history and some world history. He should be competent in arithmetic and geometry; should write and spell correctly in Spanish; know something of the fundamentals of zoology, botany, physics, anatomy, and other sciences (without laboratory work). He may have a smattering of English or another foreign language. Books in this school are supplied by the state. Learning is chiefly by rote, and the children recite in a rapid rhythm. It is probably the most efficient way to teach large classes of youngsters who must get a quick and limited education. These classes range from 40 to 69 students at full attendance!

Parochial schools are in many cases superior to federal and state schools. In view of the fact that Mexico is 98 per cent Catholic, Catholic schools have a curious status. They are called private schools and are not acknowledged as religious schools, which are prohibited by the constitution. They accept foreign and non-Catholic students, who may be exempt from church attendance and religious instruction.

Let us visit one on a hill overlooking a pretty town of the central plateau. Behind the thick gray stone walls of a former convent, students assemble on a concrete court backed by towering cypress trees. Little girls wear pretty navy-blue pinafores over white blouses, with navy-blue pleated skirts. Little boys dress in gray trousers, white shirts, and, if the day is cool, navy-blue sweaters with a white stripe on one sleeve. They march around the court and form lines, boys and girls separately. Each black-robed *madre* inspects her class for cleanliness of face, hands, uniform, and for polished shoes. She sends shining examples to the platform of honor. If more girls appear than boys, they win the use of the court for volleyball at recess. If the boys win, they play soccer—provided some child has brought a ball from home. The Mother Superior makes announcements, names honor students, if the monthly report cards have been given out, and sends the children to class.

In all but the most modern schools there is a scarcity of good equipment, but discipline and teaching skills are often very good, and the interest and attentiveness of the children excellent. In provincial schools—though there are many exceptions—a table or simple desk is shared by two, three, or even four children seated on a bench. The walls may have one blackboard, some artwork by the children, a map of Mexico, an anatomy chart, a portrait of the President, Juárez, or some figure of Mexican history. In a religious school there is a shrine or picture of the Virgin. Older classrooms may have no light except that from an open door, a single window, or, on dark days, a naked electric light bulb. However, much rebuilding is going on to take advantage of daylight with large windows.

Except for some schools in the capital, which are adjusting to summer vacations, holidays for Mexican children mean two weeks or so in May and a winter vacation from the latter part of November to the first of February, with frequent days off for fiestas and holy days. Their hours are usually from 8:45 A.M. to noon and from 3 P.M. to 5, with lots of homework. There are exams in the summer, but the major examinations for completing a grade come in November. For these, students wear their best and cleanest clothes or dress uniforms (used also for parades and special occasions).

If a child is lucky enough to finish the primary grades and enter the secondary level, he finds on the faculty many of the town's distinguished citizens. Teaching, for them, is a matter of civic duty; teachers' salaries are extremely low. A writer or lawyer may teach history and literature. The mayor's sister gives a course in Spanish composition and grammar. The butcher teaches mathematics. A language professor from an adult institution teaches English. This practice lends prestige to the faculty and often supplies a teacher much better qualified than the regular staff. But too often there is virtually no regular staff except a director, and even devoted volunteers can seldom be relied on for punctuality and regular attendance.

If a primary-school graduate is very good, a patron or a priest may stake him to further study. In large cities a high percentage of students continues in free secondary schools or prevocational schools, and a few go on to vocational schools or universities. In towns and provincial cities the chances for advanced education diminish sharply. In rural areas it's a lucky child who can finish the first six years of school, even though attendance is supposed to be compulsory. Some children simply are not within reach of a school. Others cannot be spared from home, or only for short periods, and the truancy laws have no teeth in them.

In 1963 over 6,500,000 children, youths, and adults attended classes in Mexico. Nearly 6,000,000 of these were in primary school, the equivalent of our grammar schools. But of these only about 4 per cent can expect to complete a high-school education.

The rest, about 500,000, consists of about 200,000 university students (70,000 at the National University of Mexico, 31,000 at the National Polytechnic Institute schools), 170,000 farmers studying agricultural techniques, 50,000 regional and technical school students, and 50,000 normal school students. About 500,000 of the primary-school students attend private and religious schools.

The vocational opportunities in a large city are varied and the standards higher than in a smaller city, where a primary-school graduate is considered well qualified for a fair range of jobs. Those who drop out earlier become maids, mozos, or apprentices in a trade, or perhaps they will help their families in farming or a business. An eight- or nine-year-old clerk in a store often knows the stock as well and makes change as capably as his elders.

After leaving primary grades, one girl studies teaching in normal school; another takes typing and shorthand in a commercial school. Another works in a factory. A more ambitious girl enters a government office as typist or stenographer or assists a doctor, dentist, or lawyer. Boys too may take such jobs or work in banks, hotels, restaurants, printing houses. Some farm family land as ranchers, or become mechanics, watch or radio repairmen, or apprentices to craftsmen.

A few attend an agricultural or technical school. Others

may pass an examination to attend the national military college. Here they receive a higher education and learn a trade as well as riding and military discipline. They leave with commissions as sublieutenants, spend three years in service, and then are free to continue in service or to quit to practice their new vocation. It is a great opportunity for a boy from a poor home to get an education and experience that he could get in no other way. He may even travel abroad on diplomatic assignments. Other boys are drafted into military service and attend drill on Sundays for a year.

The Mexican child accepts responsibility early and learns from his parents the chores of the household, farm, or business. Apprenticeship is a natural method of learning for him and an important part of Mexican life. A boy may be formally apprenticed and perhaps even pay a fee to learn the trade instead of receiving any salary, or he may study on a more informal basis. Under certain conditions there are regulations laid down: the boy must live in the household of the *maestro*, or must not marry for a given time, for example.

If the maestro is a mason, the boy mixes cement, carries bricks, soaks them, fetches tools; eventually he learns to pour cement, set windows, do masonry. Until he becomes a maestro himself, he is considered a *media cuchara* (half spoon), midway in the process. A boy may be apprenticed to a blacksmith, carpenter, weaver, a potter, tailor, basketmaker, or a jeweler or worker in brass, copper, and tin, depending upon his interests and the prevailing occupations in his area.

Among the aristocratic and wealthy classes, a young

man is likely to study a profession in a foreign country. Not many girls attend college or university, but the trend is changing. Most girls marry early and are too occupied with families. It has never been a tradition in Mexico for girls to have advanced education, and until this century few have had any education at all beyond a little reading, writing, music, and drawing. However, more and more girls are becoming ambitious to travel, teach, enter the diplomatic service, or go on the stage, perform on radio, television, or in the movies, become nurses, secretaries, medical assistants, librarians, or even anthropologists. The career girl has become a fixture in the Mexican scene, but she is by no means as prevalent as in the United States.

It was José Vasconcelos, Minister of Education in the 1920's under President Obregón, who gave education new meaning in Mexico. To this scholar-philosopher the word had a broad significance and included music and art as well as reading, writing, and arithmetic. It meant the teaching of instrumental and choral music to prisoners and the covering of walls of public buildings with murals that could reach Mexico's illiterate peasants as well as its middle class—and foreign tourists. It meant sending the equivalent of a missionary to the most inaccessible villages— a missionary-teacher-handyman. It was a true crusade.

The large aim was to improve the community, to reduce illiteracy, and to instill in the public a cohesive sense of nationalism and of pride in the Mexican heritage. It was a program that had to be achieved by experiment and with very little money, and it leaned heavily on amateurs and volunteer workers. Each person who could read and write was asked to teach another. Women taught their servants, and schools were improvised in the houses of workmen, 379 in the Federal District alone. One group of volunteers in Durango formed an institute, and—with a sheet of zinc for a blackboard and the ground for a schoolroom— they taught fifty-four pupils. The Railroad Dispatchers and Telegraphers, 1,500 members in all, volunteered in a body.

Most important of the activities was the corps of missionary-teachers who went out to the villages and towns. They followed principles that are being studied and used today as a pattern in the UNESCO project near Pátzcuaro —attended by students from all over Latin America—and in our own new Peace Corps.

The missionary-teacher had to identify himself with the community. It was obvious that the primitive communities, hardworking and impoverished, bound by their ancient traditions, would see no urgency about such a new fad as reading *unless* it could be made immediately fruitful and its uses directly apparent. And it had to work for adults as well as children.

The missionary-teacher had to be a resourceful man with tact, knowledge of tradition, and practical abilities (carpentry, farming, first aid, etc.), as well as a minimal education. He began by talking with the elders and persuading them of the necessity for starting a school. With their backing, he enlisted men, women, and children to gather stones, dig foundations, construct walls. The people gave pigs and chickens and food to barter for lumber, doors, and windows. Benches might be stumps of trees. A garden was laid out and a play yard, a shower bath was devised of a tin can with holes through which a boy on a ladder poured water for another's shower. Wells were dug. Eventually the school might boast a lamp for night classes, a primitive kitchen, a sewing machine, a barber's chair, a first-aid kit. The whole purpose was to enrich the community experience and make the school the heart of the village. And it worked.

Within three years a thousand such schools existed and there were 65,000 pupils. Out of its scanty funds the Ministry of Education could do no more than provide the teacher with a peso a day and sometimes a blackboard and chalk. The teacher vaccinated his people against smallpox, taught them to dig wells and purify water and make sewers, and wrote to the Agrarian Department for them about their agricultural problems. In 1925 a corps of federal school inspectors was organized, some of whose members might have had no more than three years of schooling themselves. But they were devoted, capable, and eager to pass on their knowledge.

The first cultural missions included instructors in soap-making, tanning, hygiene, physical education, agriculture, and music. The second added agronomists, a carpenter, and a domestic science teacher. In ten years each of the 18 zones of the Republic had its own cultural mission, and 75 institutes under their direction were attended by about 4,500 rural teachers. Both teachers and communities were being improved.

But this did not solve the problem of finding new teachers for the millions still to be reached. To demonstrate that even the most primitive Indian was teachable, the House for the Indigenous Student was founded in Mexico City in 1925. Lacandón, Otomí, Yaqui, and Huichol Indians—from all the tribes in Mexico students came in native garb, barefooted, in loin cloth or long shirt. These boys had never seen a light bulb or a car, never eaten with spoon or fork nor slept in a bed nor spoken any but their own Indian dialect. The project succeeded all too well. The Indians became good students, often better than the city boys, and they adapted to new ways so thoroughly that they began to disdain their own cultures and refuse to return to their tribes. They remained in the cities as clerks, mechanics, or bartenders instead of carrying their knowledge back to their people.

It became evident that the gap between the modern and the primitive world was too great to be bridged in a single leap. The best way was to train rural teachers in their own environment so that they would stay and function as leaders within their own cultural pattern. But they must bring to their people some of the elements of a better life—hygiene, improved diet, better production, an interest in the world beyond their own village.

Books were scarce. In January, 1921, Government Printing Offices under the Department of Education began issuing the classics—Homer, Sophocles, Plato, Dante, Shakespeare, Lope de Vega, Calderón, Ibsen, Shaw, Tolstoi, and Rolland—for 50 centavos each! Now bookstores line the streets of the capital and other cities, and a building in the Alameda, a park in Mexico City, houses a tremendous collection of books in Spanish and other languages.

The National Symphony Orchestra in Mexico City began giving concerts for the public. Libraries were established. The School of Fine Arts was organized, also in Mexico City. Within a year 198 small libraries had been founded, 25 model schools and a commercial school had been opened. A million copies of a primary reader were being issued and circulated. Many private schools were receiving federal aid. The federal budget nearly quadrupled. Education was free, secular, and compulsory until the age of fourteen. Mexicans were avid to learn.

Trips to Aztec and other ruins were part of the program to remind Mexicans of their awesome origins. Today during a visit to the National Museum of Anthropology on Calle Moneda in Mexico City you edge your way through rooms jammed with young scholars from seven or eight up into the teens. Some sit on little stools to sketch the pre-Columbian Tarascan dogs or an ancient flute. Others listen to a lecture on the steles of the Maya or an account of new discoveries at Monte Albán.

After forty years of campaigning, one-third of the population cannot read or write—but fifty years ago less than a fifth of the population was literate. Schooling is still a major problem, although a far larger proportion of the government's income goes to education than is the case in the United States.

There are not enough schools, not enough teachers, not enough money for good equipment or adequate salaries. Too many parents need helpers at home or the few pesos a child can earn by doing errands and chores. Too many children live too far from any school. In some cases parents resent education and think it unnecessary or harmful because it conflicts with their traditions.

But most are pleased and proud that their children understand the mysteries of printed ciphers and signs, and believe that education is the key to the future of Mexico—and of their children. Without it, Mexico stands still. With it, Mexico progresses.

The advance has been significant. There are more than 1,500 public libraries where there were none before, and

33 museums. There are night classes and a university for workers, open-air art schools, about 300 secondary schools, a school of tropical medicine, a fine school of anthropology. And the publication of books has greatly increased.

In all parts of Mexico, "instant schools," based on a prize-winning architectural design by Pedro Ramírez Vásquez, are springing up overnight or in two or three days. The basic kit, half the cost of conventional construction in Mexico, contains everything from steel girders, doors, and windows to blackboards, a small library, a radio-phonograph, and a slide-film projector. Each school when finished carries pictures of Mexican heroes, maps, or other visual educational devices. The program calls for the erection of 39,000 new school rooms by 1970.

Until recently the University of Mexico, which is autonomous, was ruled by the fickle wishes of the administering students, who could so easily be swayed by infiltrating agents of foreign powers. Faculty members were lax with their classes. Entrance standards had been lowered, and teaching and morale suffered. Under the new chancellor, the distinguished surgeon and cardiologist Ignacio Chávez, it is hoped that its scholastic achievements may rival its physical splendor and scope. The magnificent campus of the National University of Mexico on the outskirts of the city, known for its splendid modern buildings, has a history dating back to 1551.

Since about 50,000 North Americans live in Mexico, many of their children attend Mexican schools and universities, but others go to American schools in Mexico. These institutions range from a little two-room school with an enrollment of one or two dozen students of all ages to the impressive American School in the capital.

More than 3,000 foreign students each year study at Mexican institutions, many of which offer courses that are accredited in United States colleges and universities. Mexico City College is a popular institution with courses given in English and Spanish.

In spite of low salaries, many Mexican teachers are intensely devoted to their work and have a sense of mission. One couple, married, with six children, teach in a small rural school. They earn less than $50 a month between them. Yet when they find a promising student is being kept out of school to help out at home or to earn money, these two squeeze a few pesos from their tiny salary to pay the parents what the child might earn so that he can stay in school. This is dedication.

7

Mexico at Work

A mile or two beyond a grove of eucalyptus trees on the highway that passes through the State of Guanajuato, there is a ranch of some 900 acres planted in wheat, corn, sugar cane, onions, and tomatoes. The soil is rich, black, and irrigated. Water, pumped by diesel engines, gushes forth. Tractors and reapers are busy in the fields, and there are sheds to shade packers. The tomato vines are firmly staked and wired. The crops are rotated and the best seeds planted. The land is flat but surrounded by mountains in the distance, and the Río Lerma runs through the area.

This is the choice region of the Bajío, beyond the city of Querétaro, the most fertile and productive part of the central plateau and of Mexico. The lushness of the ranch and the efficiency of its operation suggest comparison with a large Middle Western farm in the United States. But in the Middle West there would be rolling hills and level prairies instead of distant mountains, and oak, elm, maple, and poplar trees instead of mesquite and eucalyptus. And the Midwestern farmer or rancher lives on his land in a trim frame house with electricity, plumbing, and all luxuries from washing machines to blenders and television sets.

Here in Guanajuato instead of a frame house there is an hacienda of stone and adobe. It was once a beautiful colo-

nial building, almost a fortress, built around a courtyard.
And a fortress it had to be, to survive banditry and revolutions. It is now occupied not by the owner of the ranch
but by employees, a few families who make no demands
about repairs or sanitation, while the owner lives in a
nearby town. The occasional hacienda that is visited or
lived in by the *hacendado* and his family is apt to be furnished with nothing but essentials—beds, tables, chairs,
perhaps a few chests and wardrobes. This is a hangover
from days when bandits or revolutionaries would gallop
up, seize what they wanted, and burn the rest.

Fifteen ranches like this, covering in all about 4,500
acres, are owned or leased by one man, in his name or in
the name of members of his family. Although about 100
million acres of farmland have been partitioned out to
campesinos since the Revolution, these acres have a way
of gravitating into the hands of more aggressive and capable men and away from the small farmers. Last year
these fifteen ranches employed about 2,000 laborers.

One of these ranches is run by a young man in his early
twenties, Ignacio León Torres, nephew of the *ranchero*.
He was tutored at home and continues to read extensively,
especially history and books on agriculture. Like many
such capable young men, he never attended college. His
father had left the ranch to his three sons, and when the
oldest one died, Ignacio took over its management at nineteen.

His cousin, Toribio Martínez, two years older, now is
business manager of the fifteen ranches for his uncle, with
the responsibility of finding good markets for the products
and making advantageous deals in purchases and sales.
His background and training were in business, not agri-

culture. A native of Celaya, he finished his schooling with two years of study in Mexico City. At nineteen he was manager of an International Harvester agency and later worked in promoting a real estate development. He has traveled in the United States and has broad and lively interests—in guns, exploring, photography, dancing, and astronomy—and has attended international conferences in astronomy.

By contrast with these prosperous ranches, there is a smaller ranch of some 450 acres near San Miguel de Allende. Here the land is stony, full of rocks, gutted with gullies. Most of it is without water except for seasonal rains and what is preserved in a season of heavy rainfall in a small dam. The only buildings are a tiny adobe hut, a couple of sheds, and a corral, and—because the Mexicans are careless about where they dump their refuse—garbage litter is scattered over an acre at the dirt road that leaves the highway. A flock of fifty goats mixed with a few sheep, an old white horse, and a little black mare with her foal stray over the scant pasturage. The farm equipment consists of a two-wheeled cart and some primitive tools.

This ranch is planted with corn, beans, squash, and a little maguey. This rancher lives in town and rides out daily on horseback to join four peons in working the land. Most of it was purchased with earnings from work in the United States as a *bracero* (agricultural laborer) and cowboy in Colorado, Wyoming, and California. The owner would like to improve his land with a better dam, irrigation, a well and pump, better seeds, more livestock. But he lacks cash, and to borrow money means paying a minimum interest of 1 per cent per month, which with penalties for late payments and various clauses might amount to as much as 18 per cent to 24 per cent in a year.

Tractors and scientific agricultural methods are not feasible on land like his, which is so pitted with rocks, ledges, and arroyos. Everything must be done by hand. Maguey, which yields mescal, pulque, fibers, and other useful products, would be a fine crop to plant. It needs no attention. The investment amounts to only about 25 cents a plant. It survives through heat, frost, and dry or wet seasons. It can thrive in poor soil, and on maturity it nets from $15 to $30 or so per plant. But planting even a thousand maguey requires an investment of $250, which the rancher can ill afford, and it means waiting eight to ten years for the plants to mature.

Goats are harder to keep than sheep because of their energy and agility, but this rancher prefers them. Wool yields only a few pesos at clipping time, whereas goats' milk, widely used to make candy and cheese, as well as for drinking, supplies a better income through the year.

Much worse off is the campesino who lives in a small village on an hacienda with a few dozen other families. He has a tiny windowless hut of adobe with a thatched roof, a small patch of land fenced in by organ cactus, where he raises a little garden produce for his family and keeps a few chickens, pigs, and goats, and he farms a milpa near the village. His land too is arid and stony, poor in topsoil, and provides a bare subsistence.

Theoretically land in the Bajío and some other regions of Mexico can produce several crops a year, and many ranchers in good locations cut as many as ten or eleven crops of alfalfa in a good year. In practice, much land is cultivated that is never harvested when the rains fail and crops are burned out. Perhaps one year in three brings enough rain.

In other parts of Mexico there are great plantations of coffee and henequen, and cotton, sugar, wheat, tobacco, and rice. In the north ambitious ranchers with more resources are building up impressive holdings with irrigation. Cotton and coffee are the leading export crops.

Mexico is confronted with an overwhelming problem. It must balance the needs for high production to support its rapidly growing population, rising at a rate of 3 per cent a year, with the needs of the individual campesino and the emotional commitment of the Revolutionary doctrine of restoring the land to the peon. High production can best be satisfied by large ranches operated by scientific methods. But more than half the population is still rural, in spite of steady migration to the cities and to industrial occupations. There is simply not enough arable land to provide even a minimal living for each peon and his family. There are still almost a million persons entitled to land who lack so much as a milpa.

Industry and agriculture have advanced enormously since the Revolution. Unfortunately, so has the birthrate. There is a constant race between growth of population and the country's ability to support itself. The population of Mexico increases at about a million a year because the birthrate continues high while the mortality rate is steadily diminishing under improved hygiene and medical care. The median age of the Mexican population is much lower than ours (eighteen versus thirty), and this means a vigorous crop of young workers. By 1970 the population is expected to pass 45,000,000.

os Voladores (The Flyers)—
everal versions of this dance sur-
ive from Aztec days. *(Mexican
Tourist Bureau)*

For nearly two centuries before the Conquest the Aztecs ruled
much of Mexico from the shining city of Tenochtitlán (here shown
in small scale reproduction). *(Hamilton Wright)*

Hernán Cortés, hero and villain of the Conquest of Mexico, 1519-1521, is the principal founder of Colonial Mexico.

Maximilian, briefly Emperor of Mexico, arrived as a puppet of Napoleon III in 1864, unwittingly precipitated civil war, was captured and executed in Querétaro in 1867.

Benito Juárez, an Indian from Oaxaca, was a contemporary and the Mexican equivalent of Lincoln and led liberal forces against Maximilian.

The nun Sor Juana Inés de la Cruz, the literary star of New Spain, is one of the romantic figures in Mexico's history.

Indians pose for a family portrait with a backdrop at the Shrine of Guadalupe outside of Mexico City. (*Hamilton Wright*)

Patio of Posada de San Francisco, San Miguel de Allende, shows characteristic fountain, arches, stonework, macetas of flowers, and bougainvillea vines. *(Lois Hobart)*

Mexican handicrafts are displayed at Museum of Popular Arts and Crafts, Mexico City *(Mexican Tourist Bureau)*

An Otomí Indian boy, as broad-faced and diminutive as his ancestors, wears huaraches and feels dressed up. *(Lois Hobart)*

The church is the heart of the Mexican village, surrounded by adobe houses and organ cactus, with the mountains beyond. *(Mexican Tourist Bureau)*

Mexicans live with the awareness of death and on the Day of the Dead, November 2, keep vigil all night to commune with their dead. *(Hamilton Wright)*

Religious pilgrims journey some two hundred miles on foot with banners and song to the shrine at San Juan de los Lagos. *(Lois Hobart)*

Happy young scholars study on a doorstep in Oaxaca in the constant crusade for literacy. *(Lois Hobart)*

A criada (maid) launders clothes at the public laundry. *(Lois Hobart)*

School children perform gymnastic feats for a celebration at Puebla. *(Hamilton Wright)*

Students cross the campus of the National University of Mexico in front of the mosaic façade of the library designed by Juan O'Gorman. *(Mexican Tourist Bureau)*

Federal agent teaches better agricultural methods to farmers in southern Mexico. *(Mexican Tourist Bureau)*

Burros, here carrying loads of wood, are an inevitable part of the Mexican landscape.

Fishermen of Michoacán use the famous butterfly nets in their quest for the delicious whitefish of Lake Pátzcuaro. (*Mexican Tourist Bureau*)

Everyone is enchanted by the variety and artistry of the straw and metal-wire woven products of Tequisquiapan, Querétaro. *(Lois Hobart)*

"Beloved and esteemed mamacita," begins an illiterate campesino, dictating a letter to a public stenographer with an ancient machine in the plaza of Cuernavaca. *(Lois Hobart)*

A jewelry salesman sets up a portable booth in Mexico City. *(Lois Hobart)*

Bullocks draw a primitive cart through a village of tropical Mexico. *(Mexican Tourist Bureau)*

In a charreada (rodeo) a charro makes the Paso de la Muerte (Leap of Death) from his bareback horse at the gallop to the back of a wild mare. *(Lois Hobart)*

The Entremeses are skits and plays by Spanish dramatists performed on the streets of Guanajuato in the spring. *(Mexican Tourist Bureau)*

A rejoneador who fights Portuguese style on a highly trained horse wears the court costume of the eighteenth century. *(Mexican Tourist Bureau)*

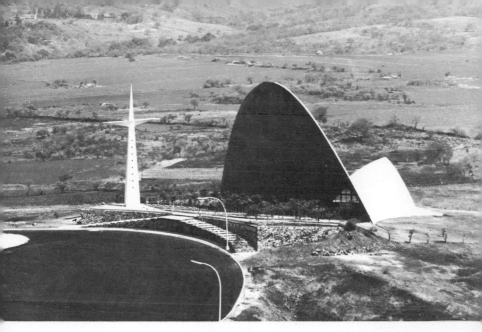

Cuernavaca is known for its charming residences and also for this example of modern architecture. *(Mexican Tourist Bureau)*

...eworks for a fiesta in front of ...e Parroquia of San Miguel de ...lende, Gto. *(Lois Hobart)*

Dancers perform regional dance before a church in Puebla. *(Mexican Tourist Bureau)*

Since before Moctezuma II, the zócalo or plaza of Mexico City has been the heart of Mexico. *(Mexican Tourist Bureau)*

The government has a perpetual battle on its hands against the vast unusable desert, mountain, and eroded areas and against the erratic rainfall and water supply. To arrest erosion and rescue the topsoil, the government has planted nopal cactus, maguey, and millions of trees, which also serve to beautify the landscape. Now hundreds of miles of highways and dirt roads are lined with young pines, and the government offers trees free to anyone who will plant them.

It is hoped that with some of the new dams and other projects under way, land can be reclaimed from swamps and flooded areas to usable farm soil. A major project is the control of the basin of the Papaloapan River in the southeast. Much has been done there in the way of flood control, sanitation, and establishment of hydroelectric plants.

Half of Mexico's people live directly from the land—but the land is not kind. Over 7 per cent is desert or otherwise unusable. About 34 per cent is still forest—pine, oak, fir, mahogany, cedar, primavera, and the chicle-yielding sapodilla. Pastureland, mostly on hills and mountainsides, accounts for some 44 per cent.

Of arable land, only 15 per cent has abundant rainfall. About 17,500,000 acres need irrigation, and 35,000,000 are "seasonal" land, which produces on the average one good crop every three years. Nature in Mexico is not cooperative, but the government is trying to harness it with irrigation, dams, and reforestation.

Even arable land does not yield what it could. More than half of it is planted in corn, but Iowa alone grows five times as much in a year. Mexico produces about 8 bushels of corn per acre—Canada 37. Wheat-sown land

yields 11.5 bushels an acre in Mexico—18.8 in Canada.
While it must be admitted that statistics in Mexico are
more uncertain and unreliable than in other countries—
because of difficulties of communication, inaccurate reports from campesinos, and other factors—there is no
doubt that the crop production is far lower than it would
be with more efficient methods.

The situation can be improved. It has slowly been realized that in most cases the Mexican farmer is better off
working cooperatively—as he did in pre-Conquest days
—than in mere subsistence farming of milpas, which do
not get a chance to recover fertility by rotation of crops.
Cooperative farmers can take advantage of pooled resources to buy or rent tractors and equipment, to select
seeds and fertilizers and use insecticides, to provide irrigation and rotate crops. They can plant avocado and orange trees, potatoes, eggplant, and tomatoes, all of which
give many times the income that corn does.

The raising of more cattle and other livestock makes better use of pasturage and adds meat to the diet of more
Mexicans. The practice of fattening cattle before slaughter,
a fairly recent innovation in Mexico, will improve the
quality of the beef. So will breeding the native stock to
imported breeds like the Hereford and Zebu. Mexico's
livestock population is among the highest in the Western
Hemisphere. It ranks second in number of mules, burros,
and goats; third in number of horses; fourth in cattle;
sixth in sheep. Such projects as that of encouraging small
farmers to raise poultry by scientific methods are spread-
ing out in increasingly wide circles to benefit more people.

The thousands of braceros who work on American
farms and ranches each year—300,000 of them before the

recent cutback prescribed by the United States government—return with new knowledge and experience of
modern farming methods and equipment. They can do
much to improve agricultural conditions in Mexico, especially if ways can be found to lend them money at less
prohibitive rates than now prevail because money is so
scarce.

In agriculture Mexico is expanding at a yearly rate of
6.8 per cent (8.2 per cent in 1958, a very good year)
and steadily outstripping the predictions of ECLA (the
United Nations' Economic Commission for Latin America). In the future, granted good agricultural years, it may
produce a surplus of food and continue exporting tomatoes,
garlic, bananas, and oranges, for instance. The national
diet should gradually improve and result in a more vigorous population.

The fishing industry could contribute more than it does
and is steadily being built up. Lower California has the
most modern packing plants, the highest overall catch,
and is one of the principal fish-exporting regions. Veracruz, Sonora, Sinaloa and Campeche are other sources of
seafood in quantity.

Industrialization is another partial answer to the race
between the high birthrate and the food supply. Astonish-
ing strides have been made. In manufacturing, the ECLA
forecast an annual rate of increase of 6.8 per cent, but the
actual increase in recent years has been 7.5 per cent. Now
it is believed that the production of cement, steel, and
other important products will reach the ECLA-predicted
levels *before* the dates anticipated. Tourism too, the most
important business of Mexico, continues to rise despite

an occasional setback during political crises and international incidents.

The forecast for the next decade appears very bright. Mexico is fortunate that, unlike most Latin American countries, her trade is diversified and not at the mercy of the fluctuations in the world market of a single product.

Manufacturing helps in the formation of a new class of consumers to add to the flourishing middle class. Industrial workers are relatively well paid, and the number of Mexicans who are buying gas ranges, electrical equipment, refrigerators, and cars, as well as smaller items, is growing. Now 16 per cent own cars, 83 per cent radios, and 24 per cent TV sets. This is of special importance because formerly the outstanding characteristic of the Mexican market has been its low purchasing power.

Although a large percentage of the rural population still makes or buys inexpensive handcrafted furniture and other articles—which, it should be noted, are sometimes cheaper and more attractive than comparable manufactured items—more and more campesinos too are being drawn into the market for manufactured products.

Many of the factories of Mexico are small family enterprises or shops which employ only a dozen or so workers, but some are huge plants. Industry employs over 1,700,000 workers. More than 1,000,000 people work in services, about 900,000 in commerce, about 275,000 in transportation. The percentage of Mexicans in agriculture has dropped steadily, but in 1959 it still accounted for more than half of the working population, or about 6,300,000.

Because of the extremely low income of the rural population, the average per capita income is about $250 a year; the farmers average only about $220 a year. The urban industrial workers average over $1,000 annually, the workers in services and communications about $1,700. Obviously country dwellers are attracted to the opportunities for greater earnings in the cities, and the shift to urban centers will continue.

Until recently all factories and plants were built around the capital and a few other large cities. Lately the trend has been to erect new ones in villages or small towns to give them new life and to alleviate industrial overcrowding from metropolitan areas.

Mexico is trying to curb the buying of costly big American-made cars in favor of smaller European and Japanese cars. Since the government subsidizes the oil industry and loses money on the gasoline sold, it naturally wishes to cut gasoline consumption by the use of economy cars. Yet the American compacts are difficult or impossible to get. The government has lowered the duties on European cars but has raised them on the American-made ones. It is, further, actively limiting the North American companies that merely assemble the automobile in Mexico, using imported parts, instead of building the entire car in Mexico. Because of the scarcity of United States cars, even old models are expensive, and thirty-year-old ones are still frequently on the road.

Mexico badly needs technicians in all fields. Instead of importing them as before from other countries to give instruction in needed skills, the program now calls for sending young people abroad to learn new skills and knowledge, bring back these assets to pass on to others, and adapt new techniques to the peculiar requirements of Mexican conditions. It is now official policy to discourage foreign technicians from staying beyond the two years allotted by the government and even to discourage foreign students from outstaying a period of five years of study. The problem is—will the young Mexican technicians return to their country or will they be tempted in too many cases to remain abroad where they can earn more and enjoy a higher standard of living?

Until midway into the nineteenth century, mining accounted for most of Mexico's foreign trade and exports. It amounted to between 70 per cent and 90 per cent at various times. It was the flow of precious metals from the mines that paid for its imports, made possible its leap into nationhood, caused the building of the railroads, and gave Mexico status in the world. Directly and indirectly, mining produced about half of Mexico's income as a colony before it gained its independence. With modern mining methods replacing the old, painful, and costly manual labor, the output in the last fifty years has equaled Mexico's mining output of the previous four centuries. About 100,-000 workers are employed.

Gold, copper, and zinc are mined. Mexico is first in world production of silver (1,385 metric tons in 1961), and high in sulphur and lead. Coal, iron, and manganese are other important minerals. Oil, once very important, has fallen off.

Mexico is attempting now to place its economy on a more solid basis than in pre-Revolutionary days. It retains more control over foreign investments, and it promotes the cooperative working of foreign and Mexican enterprises instead of bringing in large foreign staffs to establish and maintain new businesses.

The signs are healthy. Mexico's gold reserves and exports are growing. National production is thriving. Agricultural output has increased. Foreign investments are rising and Mexican investments abroad are dropping. Building is increasing. Electric power is up 40 per cent in the last five years. Mexico has the best railroad system in Latin America. Factories are turning out 9 per cent more goods this year than last year.

The peso seems to have become stabilized at 8 cents— 12½ pesos to the American dollar—since the devaluation of 1954. The Nacional Financiera, a credit institution, was founded to promote Mexican business and industry in the 1930's and has doubled its capital within a few years. There is progress, yes, but there is still not abundance.

One of the significant developments of 1960 was the formation of a Common Market—like that of Europe— by seven leading nations of Latin America, including Mexico. These nations will trade with each other at reduced tariffs which will be consistently lowered by agreement until the tariffs are minimal or nonexistent. An economic accord of this kind tends to lead to closer political bonds and to bring in more members of the economic community. This step may free the nations of the Latin American Common Market from overdependence on United States economic policies.

8

Olé!

In ancient Mexico, a really rabid ball fan might risk selling himself and his family into slavery to back his bet on the team he favored to win! The ballgames of two thousand years ago were played in a court shaped like a Roman numeral I, with a narrow central alley of slanted walls and a corridor at each end. The players propelled the ball—a *heavy* one of pure rubber about the size of today's basketball—with their hips and knees, never throwing or kicking it. The game was dangerous and sometimes fatal. The object was to pass the ball through a vertically set hoop scarcely larger than the ball itself, but since that must have been a rare accomplishment, there were probably other methods of scoring too. Even the helmets, belts, and loincloths of the players were revered, and a ball court was part of every ceremonial city. The present-day equivalent of the game, and equally beloved, is soccer. It is played in fields by children of all ages.

From the Spaniards comes the game of frontón or jai alai—from an old Basque game. It is a very fast game played on a court with three walls. Each player wears a sort of curved basket strapped to one wrist for slinging the ball. Children play a version of it as handball or with tennis rackets, and the frontón courts are popular all over Mexico.

From the United States comes *"beisbol,"* and new baseball fields are springing up throughout the country.

In tennis, Mexican players have been distinguishing themselves. In the Pan-American Games of 1959 they won the men's doubles, the mixed doubles, and the women's doubles. Two Mexicans, Rafael Osuna and Yolanda Ramírez, were ranked in the world's top ten players in 1961. In 1962 Mexico upset the favored United States team and went on to face Australia in the finals of the Davis Cup matches.

Bicycling, bowling, mountain climbing, swimming, and softball are other popular diversions.

Mexican riders have long been noted for fine horsemanship. For many years, under the leadership of Gen. Humberto Mariles, they were triumphant contenders at the Olympic Games and other international competitions. For a period, internal dissension prevented official participation outside the country. Recently an accord has been reached, and teams are now representing Mexico once more. In 1962, the team at the National Horse Show at Madison Square Garden and other competitions in the United States and Canada included: Lt. Col. Rubén Uriza, Capt. Hector Zataráin, Major Joaquín Hermida, Capt. Roger Barceló, and alternate Capt. Rafael Cervantes.

There are many active riding clubs in the capital and throughout the country. They stage jumping competitions, cross-country races over natural obstacles and through rivers or lakes, and dressage events, which are well attended.

An active cavalry helps to preserve the traditions of fine horsemanship by encouraging both military and civilian riders and competitions. Its cooperation with civilians who are interested in riding but lack money, horses, and equipment is altogether remarkable.

Officers give basic or advanced instruction to civilians (even to foreigners) at military posts. They not only lend cavalry horses for practice but even truck them to meets and plan and officiate at civilian meets. Certain posts in neighboring towns may be staffed with soldiers to care for military horses and a noncommissioned officer to train civilians. Cavalry officers also help train horses of some civilians. Probably in no other country is it possible for a novice rider to get such unusual free instruction or to ride with so little expense. Moreover, the cavalry sends troops and officers to ride in parades and celebrations and to aid in benefits through demonstrations of riding and jumping. It is a generous and farsighted policy of cooperation which pays off in fine riding and wide interest in equitation.

Also fascinating are the displays of riding in another style by vaqueros and charros. They use the elaborately adorned Mexican saddle with a high pommel instead of the flat or English saddle. The riders dress in short boleros and matching tight trousers of gray, blue, green, black, brown, or maroon, with fancy embroidered shirts and enormous sombreros decked with silver braid and embroidery. Girls and women who appear as charras ride side-saddle in elaborate dresses and large sombreros, and some in the *China Poblana* (Chinese girl of Puebla) costume, which is an embroidered white blouse and gay skirt. The charro horses are rarely large but usually are fine-looking, compact, short-bodied, arched of neck, and have flowing manes and tails.

Most large cities have a charro association which regularly holds practice sessions at neighboring ranches and occasionally a formal *charreada* in competition with a team from another city. This might be called a rodeo with a Mexican accent.

Roping feats involve stunts on the ground and from horseback. One rider ropes the steer's horns while another ropes the back legs, and the two stretch the animal between them until it falls. A third man mounts the steer on the ground. When it is released and jumps up, he rides with both hands instead of one, as our cowboys do. Another charro lassos a wild mare galloping around the ring. It should be remembered that many of our cowboy terms (reata, lariat, corral, sombrero, for example) derive from Spanish.

A popular feature is the *coleadero.* In this a bull chased by horsemen charges down a walled alley toward the ring; one rider leans far out of his saddle, seizes the bull's tail, jerks it under his right stirrup, and twists and overthrows the bull at full gallop. Many a charro who indulges once too often in this exploit loses a thumb or finger. Most spectacular feat of all is the *paso de la muerte,* the leap of death. One charro unsaddles his horse and mounts bareback, riding even with a wild mare pursued around the ring by his companions. The climax comes when the charro leaps at full gallop from his mount to the mare.

One of the most exciting events, at least for foreigners, is the performance of the charras, the girl riders. Typically, the eight members of a charra troupe, dressed in different colors, enter the ring individually at full gallop and pull up short in front of the audience with each horse forced back to his haunches. When all members have appeared, they ride through maneuvers, almost entirely at the gallop. They circle the ring first singly, then in pairs, in fours—and finally all eight abreast. Then they weave in and out by pairs, separate into two lines, and at the gallop cross lines, one horse cutting across behind the other. Sometimes a charra shows off her horse by pirouetting, making him bow or back clear across the ring. Most of these girls are in their teens. The maneuvers demand great skill, but the girls look as comfortable as if they were in rocking chairs. When one girl fainted at a perform- ance, her partner not only managed to seize her before she fell but pulled up both horses from the gallop as well.

The informal practice charreadas are sometimes even more fun to watch. *Aficionados* gather at these to watch or participate in branding, riding bulls and wild mares, roping, and so on. Music, soft drinks, beer, and punch, tacos, beans, and other refreshments are added attractions. Often four or five hundred people arrive, by horse, burro, bicycle, automobile, and even on foot.

Such scenes have changed little since Mme. Calderón de la Barca, wife of the first Spanish Minister to Mexico, described her visit over a century ago in her fascinating *Life in Mexico*. This lady, herself a talented rider, tells of one journey to the *plaza de toros* (bullring). She attended with a party of fifty who were seated upon a platform above the ring. Opposite was another platform for wives and daughters of foremen and rancheros. Nearby a small orchestra was playing. Several bulls were driven into the ring and one at a time were roped, thrown, branded, then freed and driven out. She reports:

> I saw a toreador, who was always foremost in every- thing, attempting to drag a bull by the horns, when the

animal tossed his head, and with the jerk of one horn tore all the flesh off his finger to the very bone. The man coolly tore a piece off a handkerchief, shook the blood off his finger with a slight grimace, bound it up in a moment, and dashed away upon a new venture. One Mexican, extraordinarily handsome, with eyes like an eagle, and very thin and pale, is, they say, so covered from head to foot with wounds received in different bull-fights, that he cannot live long; yet this man was the most enthusiastic of them all.

Afterwards the party sat in a tent formed of boughs hung with white moss, ornamented with red blossoms and scarlet berries. Mme. Calderón found the meat quite horrible, smelly, and tasting of smoke, but she enjoyed the boiled fowl, chile, tortillas, fruit, sweetcakes, and pulque. Later came more branding, walking in the market, a bullfight, and the return by horseback and coach to a distant hacienda for dinner and dancing. At two in the morning the same men who had been exercising so violently were still dancing the folk dances called *jarabes*. Said Fanny Calderón, born a Scot and bred to British traditions, "It beats fox hunting!"

Some Mexican diversions, like cockfights and bullfights, seem to us unnecessarily brutal. That the bullfight is gory is beyond question, but mere butchery it is not, if the matador (*torero*) and the bull are good. It is only fair to try to look at the *corrida* (bullfight) with the eyes of a Mexican and not with our prejudices.

In all major bullrings, it is a drama played according to strict rules. Everything is prescribed: the design of the arena, the weapons used, the weight and size of the bulls, the condition of the horses, the order of the matadors in fighting, the time limit on each phase—and the music, played by the band, that introduces or comments on each phase of the corrida. What cannot be prescribed are the courage, agility, grace, and skill of the torero and the bull.

For sheer pageantry the bullfight is impressive. At 4:30 P.M. the doors of the arena open. A constable on horseback leads the procession of matadors and their assistants to salute the judge and circle the ring. No costume was ever devised for a man quite as striking as the "suit of lights" (*traje de luces*) worn by a matador. It is brilliant with silver or gold embroidery, and may be made of white, green, blue, mauve, scarlet, yellow, or gray silk. The matching cape is slung over the shoulder, and the torero wears a little cap, the black *montera*, on his head.

And nothing in the world is quite as arrogant as the step of a bullfighter. Sometimes you see that it's empty cockiness and bravado based on insecurity. Sometimes you know instinctively that it's the real thing, confidence—not without humility and deep respect for the deadly opponent—born of skill and experience. And *that* can never be counterfeited. Implicit in that grave proud walk is the knowledge that death may wait in the shadows of the plaza. And the vivid bold music rings out with irresistible spirit.

Behind another door of the arena waits a bull that has been bred for this day. His whole life has been spent in play, and in mock and real battles, with other young bulls on the ranch. He has never seen a man on foot. But this day he senses that he is an instrument of death. The door opens and he explodes into the ring.

The "peons" or assistants work him with the *capote* (a cape generally used with one hand) while the torero studies the bull. He gauges its speed, its ability to stop short, to turn, its tendency to hook in one direction or another, its favored spots in the arena. Two *picadores* (mounted men on padded horses, each armed with a lance) enter, and the bull charges. After each *pick*, the matador lures the bull away. In the next phase, the *banderilleros* take their turn and place three pairs of darts in the bull's shoulders. It is always the business of the assistants to do their job without trying to rival the matador, but placing the *banderillas* is a dangerous activity. In some cases the torero himself undertakes it.

In the last phase the matador exerts himself in dominating the bull with the *muleta*, a red cloth attached to a short stick. He forces the bull into straight charges, passes the animal close to the body, and should show classic simplicity and unmoving courage. Too often instead, a mediocre torero demonstrates cleverness, flamboyance, and trickery, making the passes look good by leaning into the bull at the instant the horns pass by. Some matadors are brilliant in capework and passes, but they may fail in the "moment of truth" as they face the bull for the kill.

This is when the torero is most vulnerable. He must display the utmost courage when, having sighted the tiny spot where he must plant the sword, he then plunges in directly over the dangerous horns to sink the sword to the hilt. If the kill is perfect, he hears the thunderous *"Olé!"* The judge awards him an ear, two ears, or a tail—or all three—for a distinguished performance. The matador circles the ring, saluting the audience to the musical acclaim of the bullring while pretty girls throw flowers and presents, and men toss down wallets and sombreros. In rare instances the bull shows itself so magnificently valiant that its life is spared.

If it has been a poor fight, a messy kill, or a bull without courage, the matador is pelted with cushions, fruit, and bottles. A real aficionado glories in any corrida, but to most spectators there is nothing more repulsive or agonizing than a poor fight with a bull or a matador—or both—that lack heart. A really superb corrida demands the utmost in courage, power, and grace from animal and man and is altogether a singular experience. The thrill of this duel between man and beast is that it is a naked exposure of man's art, skill, and courage against sheer brute power and valor, with death always at stake.

Most corridas consist of three matadors fighting two bulls apiece. In any corrida, if a *rejoneador* (a mounted bullfighter in the Portuguese style) is present, he is always given the leading role. The great Carlos Arruza emerged from retirement as a rejoneador. This demands great skill and fine training, man and horse working as a unit. The horse is guided with leg pressure and responds with unbelievable precision and speed while the rider works the bull. Conchita Cintrón, a Peruvian and the finest of women matadors, was expert in both the Portuguese and Spanish styles before her retirement.

A torero is idolized, being a combination of a Hollywood movie star and a sports celebrity. In Mexico, bullfighting is the quickest and most dangerous road to fame. At every corrida a matador faces the threat of being mauled, gored, or killed. The best of them suffer under the demands of the public always to outdo themselves in grace and daring until, to satisfy their devotees, they sometimes give up their lives. It is a rare torero who bears no scars from the horns.

Children in the streets play bull-and-matador. In the country, boys "cape" heifers or sneak at night into the ranches that breed brave bulls to try their luck with a calf. They make their debut in local *tientas* (testings). During a regular corrida they often vault into the arena as *espontáneos* (spontaneous fighters) to maneuver the bull with a snatched-up cape. They are always evicted from the ring and sometimes jailed, but they risk everything on the chance that some manager will offer to train them or that some matador will sponsor them. With proper background and training, they perform in provincial arenas and—in the off season, the summer—in Mexico City. The best make their debuts under the sponsorship of a matador and acquire their own assistants. It is a spectacular but lonely existence.

At the other extreme in diversions is the purely cerebral battle of chess or dominoes. Nearly every café in Mexico has its devotees who linger during siesta hours or in the evening at sidewalk tables.

Mexico has television and radio coverage in nearly every area of the country. TV antennae top some of the poorest adobe houses. Attendance at frontón, soccer, and bullfights has greatly diminished since the advent of television. The industry is profoundly influencing Mexican life by introducing North American values, advertising, and customs. The programs are usually adaptations in Spanish of United States programs.

Movies are available even to the poorest. Usually the maximum charge for admission is 4 pesos (32 cents) and often it is less. Mexican producers make about ninety movies yearly. These are exported to Spanish-speaking countries, but few are of high quality. Among the classic exceptions is the recent *Macario*.

Mexico's favorite son is a movie actor of world renown comparable only to Charlie Chaplin. Mario Moreno, the noted Cantínflas, started as a clowning matador. He personifies the Mexican rogue, impudent but lovable, pretentious and pathetic, clumsily adroit with women, ever funny and ever touching, witty, resourceful, and talkative. Cantínflas is best known in the United States for his major role in *Around the World in 80 Days*.

Traveling circuses make the rounds of the provinces and pitch tents for one or two nights. They put up a single ring and a tattered big top, and all the performers lend a hand with lights, animals, and properties. There may be four or five elephants, two or three camels, a handful of lions and tigers. The costumes are tawdry and the ringmaster performs with the clowns, but the audiences adore everything. For all their shabbiness and forlorn glory, these little circuses often stage an excellent or original act, and the intimacy of the tiny ring favors spontaneous enjoyment.

Among the milder but beloved amusements are visits to parks. From early morning on, in Mexico City's Chapultepec Park, you find strollers wandering under magnificent centuries-old ahuahuete trees or feeding ducks and swans in the lakes. Often the lakes are filled with rowboats crowded with whole families, groups of teen-agers, young couples, or businessmen, usually singing to a guitar accompaniment. Or a family may visit the zoo, where the younger children solemnly ride ponies or are driven in goat carts, clutching octopus balloons and eating popcorn or candy, while their elders take pictures and gaze at the caged animals.

Arts and Crafts

Perhaps there has never existed a people so widely and generously endowed with the creative urge, especially in the plastic arts, as are the Mexicans. A joy in the grotesque and the comic, and in design, color, shape, and texture, is deeply embedded in their everyday and religious life.

A boy trundling a wheelbarrowful of manure to a garbage truck unselfconsciously plucks a crimson canna flower in passing to adorn his straw sombrero. To decorate a cart carrying a small statue of a saint at a humble ranch fiesta, the ranchero and his friends gather stalks of sugarcane or corn and thousands of daisies and sunflowers, and fasten them with colored crepe paper to horses and carts. On a certain Friday in Lent, people open the doors and windows of their houses to reveal shrines within, vivid with flowers, candles, oranges, and colored lights which embellish the scenes of Gethsemane and Calvary. Sometimes the shrines are equipped with ingenious devices to make the figure of Christ toil uphill bearing the cross, or the mourners move jerkily across the scene.

In a Mexican kitchen gay-colored tiles line much of the wall and cupboard space, and clay pots and pans hang in geometric designs on the walls. In every marketplace oranges, limes, tomatoes, and avocados pyramid in heaps of

gold, chartreuse, red, and dark green with scallops of
yellow bunches of bananas strung on wires above. Pottery, serapes, rebozos, and other articles are arranged in
pleasing symmetry.

The Spaniards did their best to eradicate the "inferior"
native cultures. They tried to substitute their churches
for Indian temples, their language for the varied Indian
tongues, their art for native forms. But the native character could not be erased. Subtly that character impressed
itself on the imported culture. The complexions of the
saints and the Virgin darkened when they crossed the
Atlantic. The churches became not only baroque but
highly adorned with an extraordinary blossoming of orna-
mentation surpassing any of Spanish origin with the possible exception of the architecture of Barcelona. The Catholic rites assumed a Mexican character and blended with
the ancient cults so that during a time of pagan festivals
a priest was hardly surprised to find the blood of sacrificed
turkeys upon a Christian altar.

Priests and monastic orders vied jealously in colonial days
to build the finest and most elaborate cathedrals. Each
was more bejeweled and gold-encrusted than the last, although set in the midst of clusters of adobe shacks and
huts.

Mexicans live intimately with their churches. They
lunch on the steps and bring babies and dogs to mass. For
fiestas, they adorn the churches with candles, crepe paper,
and papier-mâché figures, shoot off firecrackers and castillos, and string intricate fireworks from the steeples.
When church bells ring in Mexico, they ring with

abandon; even when a bell is so badly cracked that its resonance is gone, it may be heard clattering out over the town eighty times in succession. On January 17, St. Anthony's Day, the people bring their livestock and their pets to the priests for the blessing of the animals. Churchyards are crowded with sheep, pigs, burros, horses, rabbits, parrots, cats, and dogs. These are decked with ribbons, feathers, and crepe paper—and perhaps even dyed a fetching chartreuse or purple.

Secular architecture followed Spanish and Moorish conventions. There are arcades and arches—Gothic, Moorish, Roman, and hanging arches. There are balconies, iron-grilled doors and windows, private chapels, shallow pools, fountains adorned with tiles and flowers. The haciendas and great houses were built like fortresses, with massive walls and gates.

In the early nineteenth century came the wrench of independence. It was inevitable that the following revolutions and profound social readjustments should create an esthetic tempest and a rebirth of the arts.

The vein of folk art expressed in pottery, tiles, metalwork, and basketry, in the small figures of saints known as *estofadas*, in native sculpture has always been vital. It is clear too in the fiesta figures and miniature sugar creations of anteaters, seals, deer, sheep, and skulls for the Day of the Dead, in the toys of the markets, in the primitive murals painted everywhere—on trucks, over shops, and in saloons.

Perhaps most interesting of all are the painters of *retablos*. A retablo is a sort of thanksgiving offering to a patron saint, commissioned by the survivor (or a relative) of a grave illness or a terrible accident. James Norman has described one example in *In Mexico: Where to Look and How to Buy Popular Arts and Crafts*. It is a painting done with ordinary house paint on a piece of tin about eight by twelve inches, found in a village near Guadalajara. An Indian boy in *huaraches* (sandals), sombrero, and white clothes is shown riding the tail of an airplane, in a tile-blue sky, watched over by anxious angels. The caption reads:

> *Doy gracias a Santa María y al Señor Sagrado Corazón*. . . . On the Second Tuesday of September my son mounted the body of an aeroplane and rode thusly from Guadalajara to Mexico, a great distance. Many times he almost fell to the distant earth below, but because of the compassion of Our Mother and the Señor Sacred Heart to whom I pray to watch over my son, he was saved from death. This is offered in thanks on the 12th of September by Maria Herrera.

No respectable painter of retablos accepts a commission unless he is convinced of the authenticity of the miraculous survival. These untrained painters often convey feelingly and expressively the situations and emotions involved and make them into touching memorials. These retablos hang on the walls of country churches, together with miniature silver legs or arms that signify other thank offerings.

Another form of folk art was the decoration for ballads. A bald little man, José Guadalupe Posada by name (1851-1913), came to work in a publishing house in Mexico City during the Díaz regime as an illustrator of ballads, and quite unobtrusively he ushered in a new era of art in Mexico. His illustrations made such natural use of Mexican traditions and imagery that it was not considered polite in the French-influenced circles of society to notice them. He used the skulls and cadavers of the Day of the Dead, demons, folk lore, pilgrimages, and the events of the day in his illustrations. The *corridos* (ballads) were copiously illustrated by Posada's incisive scenes and widely circulated among the people.

One shows a servant girl chatting with the water carrier in a busy street—all are skeletons and skulls encased in costume. Another shows demons snatching a soul to hell for its sins. There is a demonstration of peasants scattered by mounted police. Others are views of the innocently hopeful new President Madero entering Mexico City, or a soldier hanged for desertion. They are never pretty subjects, but they are portrayed with directness, honesty, and vigor. Posada's interest in the people and the peasants was a foretaste of political and esthetic hurricanes to come.

In the decade following Posada's death, it was not a painter but the philosopher, José Vasconcelos, who, as Minister of Education in 1921, initiated the esthetic revolution and made it a part of government projects. Native art became not a curiosity but a point of departure for teaching, which replaced the imposed European methods. The teachers applied the early friars' methods of using imagery as a pivot of interest and motivation for children.

The important mural program began under the direction of Vasconcelos, who felt it was the most vivid way of reaching an illiterate public. There was volcanic activity in the Secretariat of Education. Here and in other public buildings immense sheets of cartoons drawn in charcoal were spread across walls and over doors. The famous trio of muralists, David Alfaro Siqueiros, José Clemente Orozco, and Diego Rivera, with their apprentices and fellow artists, have left an erratic but impressive record in buildings all over the country. They have stimulated enormous interest in the arts.

Some murals are powerfully conceived and executed. Others are mere works of propaganda, idealizing the peasant and Indian and maligning the oppressors—Spaniards, North Americans, bankers, brokers, and warmongers. At sixteen Siqueiros left a prosperous and conservative family to join the Revolution. Later he studied art at the National Academy and in Europe. He came back and added to his studies the contemplation of the ancient treasures of the National Museum and the painted walls of the saloons.

Siqueiros became active in unions, edited *El Machete,* a union paper, and was a political leader of the left who fought later in the Spanish Revolution with the Republicans in the 1930's. He began searching for the colonial and folk bases of his country's esthetic traditions, to incorporate them into his own work. Then he added social meaning and realism, with effects of boldness and caricature. Still politically active, Siqueiros is currently in jail for inciting students to riot. In typically Mexican fashion he is permitted great liberty in continuing his painting and receiving visits from his family.

Born in Jalisco, Orozco studied at the National Academy and was told he was a mere caricaturist and could not draw. A caricaturist he was, this man of thick-lensed glasses, fierce mustache, and business suit—but more. He was a painter of tumult and fire and subtle powerful color range. He could parody the hammer and sickle of Communism with crossed fork and knife and paint the majesty and tragedy of revolution. For his series of sketches of war he has been styled a Mexican Goya.

For years the massive bulk of Diego Rivera at work on murals in the Palacio Nacional was one of the sights for tourists. His life was a series of adventures almost as picturesque as his tales of it. Fitfully he was a Communist and honored guest in Moscow. Yet he invited Trotsky to take refuge in Mexico and strenuously protested against Russian proletarian art. During the Revolution he was in Europe, where he met Siqueiros, but he came back in 1921 more revolutionary than the Revolutionists. He painted the peon, the movie star, and the Mexico of the Aztecs. In crushing distortions he vilified the representatives of capitalism, the Church, the Conquest, and even his sponsor Vasconcelos. In the garden of his house at Coyoacán and in his studio he amassed a matchless collection of native sculpture and treasures, which were given, after his death, to his country.

Many other painters could be named, from Frida Kahlo (Rivera's last wife) and Francisco Goítia to Jean Charlot, and Miguel Covarrubias. There is the elderly Dr. Atl, critic, writer, labor organizer, and mountain climber. There is the Guatemalan Indian Carlos Mérida, who studied in Paris with Modigliani and Picasso, yet kept his own serene and individual concepts and approach to painting, with reflections of the Mexican people in their fields, homes, and mountains.

The major figure of Mexican painting now is Rufino Tamayo. Like Carlos Mérida, he has worked as a muralist but is primarily an easel painter. He is the least nationalistic of Mexican artists. He uses a subtler palette, freer, less literal forms, and is more cosmopolitan, though he is an Indian of the south. He is against the "artificial display of folklore, revolution, and propaganda," against the merely picturesque. Though he is not considered one of the Revolutionary painters, he has his own concept of what is revolutionary.

"The revolutionary painter is he who tries to find through his painting new forms of expression," says Tamayo. He searches for the essence rather than the superficial reality of Mexican subject matter. He looks for the national accent which survives not only in the remnants of ancient art and architecture, but in the typical uses of proportion, balance, and preference for certain colors, and in the persistent dualities of joy and tragedy which form so strong a current in Mexican art.

Unlike the muralists, Tamayo is not a fighter in the sense of being a propagandist. But he is articulate, though he believes that the main impact of his philosophy should be carried not by words but by his painting. In his mind, nationalism, recoiling from outside influences, hinders full development of an artist or a nation. He perceives a strong kinship between ancient art and the modern tradition, both of which escape from the severe strictures of the model and use it to provide artistic ideas or themes rather than form alone.

None of the prominent younger artists offers the promise of a young Tamayo or Orozco so far. They have been prone to follow the path of the nationalistic muralists who did so much to raise the prestige of Mexico and give it a sense of identity. Or they tend to echo the young Spanish painters or the American schools. It is time now for them to depart from too literal dependence upon superficial national traditions and themes and become less provincial in their approach, less dedicated to perpetuating their masters. It is a hopeful sign that two of the leading younger men, Juan Soriano and José Luis Cuevas, have sounded a call away from nationalism and toward a more universal expression.

Many foreign artists, drawn by centuries of achievement in architecture and art, find Mexico a sympathetic country to live and work in. Mexico City is full of art galleries, but the Bellas Artes remains the grand showcase of Mexican art. The beautiful Alameda, the park nearby, is the site of outdoor sculpture shows.

Other art schools and galleries thrive outside the capital. In Taxco there is a small art school. The more noted Instituto Allende in San Miguel de Allende attracts students from Latin America, Canada, and the United States. Recently, foreign artists living there have inaugurated an annual exhibition with the aid of the Instituto Allende, Mexico City College, and the Mexican-North American Cultural Institute. They have had much success in showing the works of promising Mexican and foreign artists residing in Mexico, and they hope eventually to include works from other Latin American artists and to show a selection in other countries. Also in San Miguel, the Instituto Nacional de Bellas Artes (INBA) has restored a handsome colonial building as a center for a small museum and for the teaching of arts and crafts.

Architecture in Mexico is currently in a livelier, more adventurous state than the plastic arts. Most striking are the varieties of texture and materials and the lavish use of plants and trees. There are scalloped walls, draperies of living greenery and vines, innumerable types of stone, brick, and cementwork, imaginative use of color, glass areas, murals, and balconies. These are seen not only in public buildings and private dwellings but in humble structures like frontón and tennis courts of reinforced concrete and wire-mesh walls, public laundries, and highway stands, as well as in churches, schools, hospitals, and museums.

The architect Luis Barragán initiated the contemporary planned residential development outside the capital known as the Pedregal. Enrique de la Mora created the modern church of steel, cement, and glass in Monterrey. Mies van der Rohe, though of course not a Mexican, and Felix Candela have also built handsome structures for factories and warehouses. Spanish-born Candela was the engineer and Jorge González Reyna and Rafael Arozarena were designers of the beautiful cosmic-ray laboratory at University City on the outskirts of Mexico City. Juan O'Gorman designed the monumental mosaic-walled library. Mexican architects have been particularly successful with huge projects like the new multimillion-dollar Medical Center, also on the fringes of Mexico City, multiple housing units, and the superbly exciting University City.

A mural in the temple of Bonampak, a ruined Maya city, shows an orchestra with trumpets, flutes, and ocarinas. Musical instruments have been recovered which indicate that even more ancient tribes knew chords, harmony, and five-, six-, and seven-tone scales two hundred years before harmony evolved in Europe. Indians used drums, whistles, flutes, ocarinas, trumpets, shells, and rattles but had no stringed instruments. One flute found can produce as many as seventeen sounds. An ocarina has been discovered in the shape of a squat little dog about three inches long. The key is changed by moving the mouthpiece farther into the mouth.

To Spanish ears, accustomed to the dulcet sounds of stringed instruments, the piercing music of the Aztecs sounded like the devil's work, and the Church fathers banned it. Instead they founded schools to teach violin and guitar to the natives. The students were so apt that in two months they learned what Spanish students learned in two years.

What we know of Aztec music is chiefly through conjecture. In some measure it has been used as a basis for certain modern compositions, like Candelario Huizar's *Oxpanitztle*. This was written to celebrate an Aztec festival and ranges in feeling from the savagery of human sacrifice to the tenderness of a flower dance. In pre-Conquest days composers and players of music were members of the staff of a palace. Singing and dancing were part of the ritual of all celebrations and much used in magic rites. On long trips travelers carried with them instruments to while away the time.

Music is still part of the daily life of most Mexicans. Not only does a guitar appear at almost any gathering, but even on a bus a musician is likely to join the travelers with a guitar and play a few songs. In the markets are mariachis and marimba players. Nearly every village has its orchestra or band for concerts on Sunday evenings at the time of the weekly promenade. In the Plaza Garibaldi in the capital, and in some other cities, the mariachis appear in their charro costumes, waiting to be hired for private parties or serenades. Alas, equally popular are the murderously loud jukeboxes in restaurants and saloons.

Corridos recount the events of the day and tell stories

of heroes and bandits, catastrophes, and tragic love affairs. A famous one is *"La Peregrina"* (The Wanderer), written for an American journalist, Alma Reed. She was to marry Felipe Carrillo Puerto, reform Governor of Yucatán, but he was betrayed by enemies and shot before the marriage could take place.

Some ballads describe the defeat of the French at Puebla in 1862. Others sing of the assassination of Madero, the pursuit of Pancho Villa, or the treacherous killing of Zapata. This is history and news events told in music for the illiterate thousands.

Mexico has its share of musical talent. The popular composer Agustín Lara, the popular singer Pedro Vargas, operatic stars Angela Peralta (no longer living) and José Mojica, and the conductor and composer Carlos Chávez have enjoyed worldwide fame.

In pre-Conquest days everyone danced, from children to nobles and priests. All wore their finest clothing and adornments, flowers, plumed headgear, and rattles. Some dances demanded great skill. For instance, a man would dance while he supported another on his shoulders who in turn supported a third on his. This three-story performance was so awesome that the Spaniards believed the devil was an invisible aid.

The friars turned the Indian love of dance, music, and pageantry to good account by modifying traditional legends and lore to represent Biblical and religious stories in a mixed form, a sort of dramatic, musical, dance pageant.

The most spectacular dance surviving from pre-Conquest days is *Los Voladores*, the flyers. A straight tree trunk as tall as a five-story building is set in a deep hole in the plaza, and five men climb to a tiny platform at the top. All wear headdresses and costumes of feathers to simulate hawks. The captain wears a red shirt and a white diagonal band on his trousers. While he dances on the platform and plays the flute and drum, the other four rope themselves to the pole and leap off. As the rope unwinds around the pole, they seem to be flying down to the ground. At the end, the captain slides down a rope without ceasing the playing of his instruments, to arrive simultaneously with the birdmen for a brilliant finale. This and other versions of the dance can be seen in the states of Veracruz, Hidalgo, San Luis Potosí, and in others on special occasions.

The *Concheros* (Shell Dancers) are far more numerous. They include men, women, and children in an organization of many thousands throughout the central plateau. They are subject to firm discipline, and in case of sickness or death in a member's family they are obliged to help each other. On their ankles they wear shells to make a tinkling sound at every movement. Their headdresses are plumed and adorned with beads and bits of mirror. Many wear long satin capes in bright reds, blues, greens, and purples. They dance in honor of the four winds and also of the *mesa santa* (communion table). The dance is said to have originated during a battle near Querétaro.

In 1531 the Spaniards came with their allies to a hill near Querétaro to conquer the Chichimecs of the region. The native chief, aware of the might of Spanish weapons and cavalry, proposed that each side fight without arms for a day to determine the winner. So on July 25 there raged a strange battle, Indians against Spaniards, fighting with fists, feet, and teeth as weapons. During the battle a shining cross and the image of St. James is said to have appeared in the air. The Indians, awed by the sight, not only promised to accept Catholicism but celebrated their defeat by dancing.

The Yaqui Indians have their deer dances, and other tribes have similar little danced dramas. Stories of the Conquest, slightly garbled, are danced and acted by the famous feather dancers of Oaxaca. In these a little girl plays La Malinche as a friend of Moctezuma rather than of Cortés and his men. Another dance represents the struggle between the Moors and the Christians. In most of these there is much clowning and frequently a devil. Some dancers, like *Los Locos*, the mad ones, wear grotesque masks and costumes, made of anything from top hats and tuxedos to clown dress, and are dedicated to foolery.

The national folk dance is the *Jarabe Tapatío*, which developed in Guadalajara and has been danced by the famous Pavlova and La Argentina. The girl wears the china poblana and the man dresses as a charro. It is a dance of heel-and-toe rhythm and ends with the rousing music from the bullfight.

In the area around Veracruz dances are announced at sunset with the whish of rockets into the sky. Men choose their partners in silence by presenting themselves, raising their hats, and turning to the dance floor. If the girls wish to accept, they follow. A man who wants to cut in on a girl on the dance floor places his hat on her head. If she prefers not to change, her partner removes the hat. Sometimes two rivals begin a verbal duel in song. One may insult the girl, who apparently hears nothing and just continues dancing while her partner defends her. If the rivalry becomes really heated, it may be settled off the dance floor with machetes.

In the bottle dance, both the man and the girl dance for a while, drink from a bottle of tequila, set it on the floor, dance over it by turns, and must sip whenever it is touched. Sometimes the dance ends rather frantically.

The *Sandunga* is danced by the Tehuanas, the reputed beauties of southern Mexico. They wear short blouses, long full skirts, and a fortune in gold coins on chains around their necks. In most Mexican dances planned for couples, the man and woman dance without touching, the woman usually with downcast eyes.

The internationally famous Ballet Folklórico of Mexico City makes use of folk dances and native dances of such tribes as the Yaquis, or the dance of *Los Viejitos* (the little old men), comic roles enacted by young clowns. On January 21, 1961, to celebrate the birthday of Ignacio Allende, the company set up a platform in San Miguel de Allende in front of the parroquia by the plaza, with lighting and sound equipment supplied by a truck. The dancers performed to the astonishment of a large portion of the audience—campesinos who had never heard of ballet but were open-minded about this odd performance because it was, after all, approved by the priest. Even rain did not dampen the enthusiasm of the audience or dancers.

Mexicans are avid for all aspects of culture. They welcome a Pablo Casals Festival at Acapulco, or visiting ballet and theatrical companies, or listen to Stravinsky conducting the National Symphony Orchestra. New art galleries spring up. Orchestras and chamber music groups tour the republic. Bookstores are everywhere and full of inexpensive literature.

A national repertory theater has been organized, with directors, actors, and set designers. The first season includes plays by modern authors from Christopher Fry to

Ionesco. *Las Alas del Pez* (The Wings of the Fish), by
Fernando Sánchez Mayans, is a play of real stature which
has toured the provinces and been translated into English,
French, and Dutch.

Newspapers like *Excelsior* and *Novedades*, magazines
like *Jueves, Mañana*, the *Revista de la Universidad de México*, and the English language *Mexico This Month*, and
informative travel bulletins are flourishing. A journalistic
tradition is growing up, and Mexico is emerging as a cultural entity and not a mere borrower from European literature and art.

Long before the advent of the Spaniards the Indians had
their literary beginnings:

> This is the account of how all was in suspense, all
> calm, in silence; all motionless, still, and the expanse
> of the sky was empty.
> This is the first account, the first narrative. There
> was neither man, nor animal, birds, fishes, crabs, trees,
> stones, caves, ravines, grasses, nor forests; there was
> only the sky. . . .
> Then came the word.

So begins the *Popol Vuh*, sacred writings of the Maya.

Of individual pre-Conquest writers, Nezahualcoyotl
(Fasting Coyote), the fifteenth-century poet-king of Texcoco, was the most noted. At eight he saw his father killed
by assassins and invaders of his kingdom. He himself escaped with the help of his tutor and became a refugee.
He was a scholar, poet, hunter, ballplayer, and courtier.
When he regained his father's kingdom after evading
many attempts on his life by rivals, he made Texcoco a

center of music, poetry, scholarship, and crafts. He built aqueducts, irrigation systems, and dikes and inaugurated a commission of arts and letters which encouraged the arts with awards and denounced or punished those guilty of poor craftsmanship and inferior performance. He believed in an unknown god rather than in the Mexican hierarchy of gods, but he permitted his people the ways of worship of their ancestors.

On a visit to one of his chiefs, he fell in love with his host's intended wife and sent the chief off to be killed in war. After a suitable interval he married the girl and by her had two sons. One, Nezahualpilli, succeeded his father in 1472 and ruled well until his death in 1516.

With the Conquest came one of the most enchanting and valuable popular histories of literature. *The Chronicles of Bernal Díaz de Castillo* was written by one of the soldiers of the Conquest fifty years later. Except for minor inconsistencies, it is written in astonishingly accurate detail, full of color, vigor, and wonder, rich in description. It is a firsthand account, crisp with dry—perhaps unconscious—humor, alive with admiration of Cortés, Doña Marina (La Malinche), and Moctezuma, full of the ailments, complaints, tribulations, and triumphs of the veteran of hundreds of campaigns.

About the time Bernal Díaz wrote his *Chronicles,* a child of pitiful physique and great talent was born in New Spain. This was red-haired Juan Ruiz de Alarcón y Mendoza, short, ugly, and hunchbacked. After studying law in Mexico, he left for Spain, embittered because his deformity prevented his appointment as a judge. In Spain he became a playwright and jurist, but he suffered ridicule for his elegant manners and his ugliness. His work shows no imprint of Mexico, but it differs from other plays of the period. The form of comedy is more closely worked out. The characters are believable and display moral principles. His plays, *Even the Walls Have Ears, How to Win Friends, The Liar*, and *A School for Suitors*, are comedies of character which resemble modern works.

Most appealing and extraordinary of all literary colonial figures was Sor Juana Inés de la Cruz. She was born in the second half of the seventeenth century in a farmhouse not far from the capital. At three she learned to read; she refused to eat cheese because she believed it would make her stupid. At six or seven, already accomplished at women's occupations of sewing and housework, she begged to be dressed like a boy and sent to a university. One tutor taught her Latin grammar in twenty lessons. When she went to live with her grandfather in the capital, the cultured wife of the Viceroy heard of her charm, beauty, and learning. Juana became the favorite lady in waiting at court. In a public examination by intellectuals she defended herself "like a royal galleon beating off the attacks of a bunch of rowboats."

Possibly she had an early disappointment in love, or perhaps her situation was made uncomfortable by the taint of illegitimacy or the attentions of the Viceroy or his courtiers. In any case, at eighteen Juana became a nun in the convent of San Jerónimo. Her cell became the rendezvous for the most distinguished people of the land. She collected a library of four thousand volumes and studied astronomy and music. She wrote verse and secular and religious plays, made comments on laws of nature based on her observations of children playing with tops or on her studies of the walls and ceiling of her room.

Even convent walls could not bar jealous criticism. Juana was censured for her writing and for being insufficiently religious. She answered the criticism with a brilliant defense of womankind in a touching biographical sketch, *Answer to Sister Philotea*. But the disapproval marked her. Eventually she sold her books, music, and instruments, and donated the proceeds to charity. In her own blood she wrote a testament of faith. During a plague she nursed the sick, caught the infection, and died at forty-four.

Except for the historian-statesman Lucas Alamán of the nineteenth century, no writer of outstanding stature appeared until the modern movement began. Ignacio Manuel Altamirano, an Indian follower of Juárez, wrote of his own life and people in *Christmas in the Mountains*, a significant departure from polite literature. The Mexican poet Manuel Gutiérrez Nájera founded the *Revista Azul* in 1894. This curtailed his own writing but encouraged other young writers.

The Revolution of 1910 gave impetus to a new literary thrust of pure Mexican flavor, full of scenes and themes of tumult. *The Eagle and the Serpent* by Martín Luis Guzmán in the next decade of the twenties tells the adventures of Pancho Villa in gory detail. The masterpiece of Revolutionary novels was *The Underdogs*, by the soldier-physician-novelist Mariano Azuela. The Indian now appears in literary work not for local color but as a primary force and the focus of attention. It is a journalistic literature, crowded with action and reporting, and the pistol becomes the symbol of fate.

One of the great literary figures of Latin America is Alfonso Reyes (1889-1959), poet, diplomat, scholar, critic, and classicist, who spent much of his life as a diplomat away from Mexico but returned and was made head of the Mexican House of Spain, a publishing house in Mexico City. In this office he assisted Spanish writers and artists in exile. *Vision of Anáhuac* and *Cruel Iphigenia* are among his works.

José Vasconcelos (1882-1959), statesman and historian, has also been very influential. Among other books he wrote the autobiographical *Creole Ulysses.*

Of the younger writers, Octavio Paz is the most eminent, of international reputation. He too is remarkably versatile—poet, essayist, critic, playwright, and diplomat —noted for his *The Labyrinth of Solitude.* Carlos Fuentes, a founder of the *Mexican Review of Literature* and a fellow of the Mexican Center of Writers, has recently achieved a great success with his fine novel, *Where the Air Is Clear.*

A recent innovation to be watched with interest is the Center for the Experimental Arts in Mexico City, founded in August, 1961. The Center proposes to bring bilingual performances of plays or readings from the literature of other nations. It will present also painting and sculpture, music, dance, and films of these nations. Its first project was a presentation of Synge's *Riders to the Sea,* and a three-month cycle which included readings of Irish short stories on the radio, lectures in the Bellas Artes and Benjamin Franklin Library about Ireland; films on Ireland and the famous Abbey Theater; readings from Irish poets; and as a finale, the first Spanish presentation of Brendan Behan's *The Hostage.*

10

From Burros to Bats

Animals are a part of a Mexican's life to an extent that bewilders American city dwellers. Burros, pigs, goats, sheep, and cattle are frequently seen on the streets of all but two or three large cities. Even in Mexico City one sees horsemen trotting serenely along a bridle path in the middle of the traffic of the Paseo de la Reforma or in Chapultepec Park. In the cities horses and burros and mules are commonly kept in stables adjoining the house in a rear patio. Rural life has no exclusive claim on them, and a townsman might find a burro or horse as indispensable as does the campesino living on an hacienda.

Certainly the most enchanting beasts associated with Mexico are the burros. The fuzzy newborn foals are about as big as a good-sized dog. They come in colors ranging from near white to shades of gray, beige, brown, or black, with a lighter underbelly. They never grow large, but they bear unbelievably heavy burdens and are remarkably surefooted and therefore useful for rough terrain all over Mexico. Tiny of hoof, large of eye and ear, they trot along at a queer, stiff-legged gait, looking straight ahead. A man mounted on a burro, sitting on its bare haunches with his feet dangling almost to the ground, at a distance appears to slide along the landscape.

The burro, imported by the Spaniards, is a great boon.

It bears riders, as well as all manner of inanimate burdens, and is a pet besides. Because it is commonly used with the most rudimentary harness and generally without any bridle, it is guided by tapping a stick on its neck or haunch and is urged along with constant kicking and cries of *Ahhhhh, burrrro!* Since it cheerfully devours anything from paper to leather or cactus, it is easy to maintain. In towns it likes to graze along the streets on weeds and grass growing between the cobblestones, and burros constitute a frequent hazard to motorists by blocking the roads. Since colonial days burro and mule trains have been a regular feature of the Mexican landscape.

Burros often show more intelligence than horses. One little filly learned to unlock the door of the tackroom near the stable by turning a key to get at the feed inside. When her owner thought to outwit her by hanging the key from the handle by a string, she promptly learned to insert the key in the lock and continued her robberies. Then she added to her sins by unbolting the stable doors to free the horses.

The typical Mexican ranch horse is small, agile, surefooted, scrawny but sturdy, most often bay, a sort of reddish brown. These are the *corrientes*, ordinary horses. The beautifully trained charro horses are somewhat larger, usually 14 or 15 hands high, and often extremely handsome with their arched necks and showy gaits. They must not be too tall because otherwise their riders cannot perform some of the charro feats. The *chaparro* is a miniature horse, which is now being exported to the United States for the use of children.

Horses ridden by cavalry troopers are large husky corrientes with great stamina but little beauty. Many of the

horses used as jumpers by cavalry officers have thorough-
bred or Arabian blood, and are taller, longer-legged, and
often beautiful.

Dogs, once raised by the Indians for food, are still
present everywhere. In the cities one often sees handsome
pedigreed dogs, but in the country they are apt to be
skinny, yellow of eye and dingy of coat, and sharp of
bark.

In the north are wild animals common in certain regions
of the United States—the pocket gopher, deer, wildcat,
fox, opossum, rabbit, hare, skunk, bear, badger, coyote,
iguana, kangaroo rat. The more exotic animals seen in
zoos come mainly from the south or along the coasts.

Tropical birds flourish, from the flamingo to the parrot
and toucan. The colorful quetzal bird, whose feathers
made it such a prize to the Indian feather artists before
the Conquest, still survives in the jungles of Chiapas and
Yucatán.

Among the sea creatures which challenge interest are
the manatees, the sea cows of the Caribbean coast. They
are ugly gray beasts, lazy, tame, and amiable, that feed on
sea grass. It's hard to imagine that these were the source
of the legends about mermaids. They give birth to one
offspring at a time. Native fishermen declare that when a
mother is seen holding two babies, as occasionally hap-
pens, she is literally baby-sitting for another manatee
diving for lunch.

Spider monkeys and howler monkeys, both with pre-
hensile tails, are found in southern Mexico. Spider monkeys
are small, thin, scraggly of hair, with naked faces and
thumbless hands. They move in troops through the forests

and feed on leaves, green nuts, and fruits. The howler monkeys are larger and more impressive, with beards and protruding features. Their longish fur is black, brown, or golden brown. They too move about in crowds, led by a big male, trundling through the trees faster than a man can run below. One howler can make a most extraordinary racket that sounds like faraway thunder combined with the roaring of dying jaguars.

Another tree dweller is the kinkajou, sometimes miscalled honey bear. It is a little animal with short, soft ginger-colored fur edged with yellow, or gray edged with silver. It eats fruits, leaves, green nuts, fungus, and any small animal it can catch, besides insects. It adores honey and alcoholic liquors. When drunk, it will go mad and attack anyone with tooth, claw, and tail.

When a Mexican speaks of *el tigre*, he means the jaguar. It is a gorgeously marked feline with ringed spots of black and gold, the largest big-game cat of the Western Hemisphere. Although it never attains the size of a tiger, the jaguar is heavier in build and may weigh as much and be almost as majestic. It is a fine tree climber but versatile enough to live on prairies and semideserts or in rocky mountains. Unless it is provoked to battle, it is quiet. All animals fear it, since it is faster than the deer. Only big bulls can face it without terror.

The hunter Pablo Bush Romero reports the result of one encounter between a bull and a jaguar. The bull weighed over half a ton; the jaguar was between ten and fifteen years old and about six feet long. The fight lasted over an hour. A radius of more than a third of a mile of trampled bushes, small trees knocked down, and thick trails of blood marked the progress of the battle. At the end of it the bull lay dead, and the jaguar, gored through the shoulder and wounded many times, was expiring 75 yards away.

Bobcats, ocelots, pumas, and smaller spotted cats are common. It is not unusual for an Indian to appear at the door of a city house with the query, *"Quiere comprar un gatito?"* (Do you want to buy a kitten?) When he opens a squirming sack for inspection, at the bottom is a tiny wildcat snarling and striking. Another passing campesino may unbutton a bulging shirt to disclose a tiny coyote cub for sale. The *jaguarondi*, mostly gray, dark brown, or red, is a less common catlike beast.

Among the odder Mexican mammals is the Central American tapir (*anteburro*). It is roughly the size of a small donkey, dark brown with a fringe of white around its ears and lips, and sometimes on throat and chest, with piglike bristles. Normally it is a retiring animal, but it is well muscled and can be dangerous if disturbed. It is amphibious and can submerge for long periods. Surveyors are grateful to the tapir because it has the ability to find paths over mountainous terrain that usually make the best possible routes for roads.

Another piglike animal is the peccary, a reddish-brown creature with a large snout and a white mustache, much smaller than a tapir. Peccaries travel in throngs over the forest floor and can be extremely dangerous. They silently surround a victim, animal or human, and then close in for the kill. If the victim attempts to escape by climbing a tree, they patiently gnaw down the tree. They are quite as fond of meat as of vegetables and fruit.

The armadillo or *tatú* is a strange animal found on open plains, in stony areas, and in wet forests. It is encased in an armor of shell and looks clumsy, but it is a prodigious digger and can also travel fast when alarmed. It bears four young at a time, all of the same sex.

Anteaters are found in tropical areas and subsist—quite reasonably—on insects. The giant anteater attains a length of six feet. When it stands on its hind legs, its heavily muscled forearms and claws become deadly weapons, and other animals, even jaguars, give it a wide berth. To feed, it sticks its long pointed muzzle into termite or ant nests or ripped-up logs and flicks up insects with its foot-long tongue. And the legend that it uses its bushy tail to sweep insects together is true.

The sloth is a slow-moving arboreal animal about the size of a large domestic cat, covered with coarse shaggy fur. It hangs from branches by its claws and moves upside down, carrying its young on its chest. Sometimes the animal is covered with parasites, which make it seem green and blend with the surrounding leaves. Despite its sluggishness, it can strike in a slashing swing with tremendous speed, bite ferociously, and survive incredible wounds.

The coatimundi is a raccoonlike animal with a long nose that can twitch to a forty-five-degree angle. Its tail is long, its legs short, and its ears small, and it has curious facial markings. It is very community-minded and travels in large bands that invade a territory and comb it completely for food, which means almost anything edible. When one turns belligerent, it is abandoned by its fellows as a hermit coati (*tejón solitario*), dangerous to friend and foe alike. A large one can finish off a dog much larger than itself with its claws and teeth. However, most are amiable and make good, clever, but mischievous pets.

Most appealing is a squirrel-shaped animal with a foxy

face called the *cacomixtle*. It has large eyes and ears, a bushy black-and-white tail, and markings on its face. Its fur is soft and dense. It is nocturnal, nimble, and extremely elusive; it can hide in the tiniest cracks of trees. Normally a tree dweller, it can live in open desert and in houses and parks. It is, says Ivan T. Sanderson, author of *Living Mammals of the World*, an escape artist that can squeeze through incredibly small openings and knows how to open anything but a padlock with its minute claws. It is savage, and feeds on birds, insects, worms, fruit, and even burrows after pocket gophers.

The tayra resembles a weasel. It varies in color according to climate and terrain, but is equally at home in trees or on the ground, and can race through the treetops. In Mexico it tends to have longer fur and a less bushy tail than the tayra of South America, and is usually dark brown with a scattering of gray.

A homely little animal called the coendou, a form of porcupine, is a real oddity. Its short spines are overlaid with thick black hair, and it has a naked, scaly tail. Normally amiable, if molested it takes a battling stance upon its hind legs and tail and growls over its clenched fists. By habit it is nocturnal and arboreal. It makes a good pet, quite docile, affectionate, and intelligent, except that it is ingenious about escaping from cages.

The paca is a rodent which can be an aggressive fighter. Its senses of hearing and smell are acute, and it is enormously fast. It somewhat resembles a very large rat with odd markings and a Roman nose. Surprisingly, it too makes a good pet—as well as a good substitute for a garbage disposal unit, since it eats practically anything edible.

The agouti, which is related to the paca, is more timid.

It is more delicate in build, has longer legs, and is very dexterous with its fingers. It can climb or swim and is capable of extraordinary leaps over chasms.

Among the more repulsive inhabitants of Mexico are such creatures as rattlesnakes, scorpions, alligators, and vampire bats. The tiny scorpions near the coasts in tropical areas are more apt to be dangerous than the larger ones of the mountains and plateaus. The vampire is a disagreeable character with an ugly snout, outsized ears, and vicious little tusks for inflicting wounds. It feeds exclusively on the blood of other animals, especially on humans and horses, and it carries rabies and other fatal diseases.

An excellent representation of the wild life of Mexico can be seen in the fine zoo in Chapultepec Park in the capital, along with animals from other parts of the world. This zoo of only 15 acres is small compared with those of San Diego or the Bronx or Washington, D.C. But its attendance record is remarkable. On Sundays it welcomes 80,000 visitors (record attendance at the 196-acre Washington zoo is 85,000), and on two successive holidays 258,000 and 191,000 visitors were counted.

It houses more than 1,700 mammals and birds. One of the most interesting spectacles is the cage that houses Princesa, a Bengal tiger, and her companion Principe, a big mongrel dog. They were suckled by the same bitch and brought up together, with the dog attaining his full size earlier than the tigress, though she now dwarfs him. They have remained great friends and play together with abandon. When Principe is let out of the cage several times a week, the tigress paces up and down fretfully until he returns for a frolic. He has even been known to snatch food from her without punishment.

The wild life of Mexico has not changed radically since the Conquest, but most of the country's domestic animals were brought by the Spaniards—goats, sheep, cattle, burros, mules, and horses. Now it is impossible to conceive of the Mexican landscape without these creatures.

Hunting in Mexico is not the plush luxury sport that it is in Africa, where a safari for a month may cost $5,000 and provide comfortable tents, bedding, food, and transportation, with protection by the professional hunter. Safari-type hunts are offered, of course, with guides, callers, dogs, and fancy equipment. But more often sportsmen simply drive to the jungle or up to the mountains with a jeep and a few supplies, hire a guide, and set off.

Usually they ride horseback or burro or go on foot through jungle, cactus, desert, and swamp. They brave swarming insects, snakes, insufficient food and drink, inclement weather without much protection, and the constant hazard of unforeseen circumstances, which in an African safari are reduced to a minimum. The wild life in Mexico is less in evidence than in Africa, where the traveler commonly sees wild herds in the open or at water holes from the truck, jeep, caravan, or auto. In Mexico the game is usually tapir, peccary, jaguar, ocelot, bear, deer, duck, or desert sheep.

The Indians have some unique methods in hunting. One neat trick is a way to capture turkeys roosting in a tree. The hunter circles under the tree while the fowl keeps twisting its neck to watch the performance until it gets so dizzy that it falls to the ground.

The Tarahumara Indians of southern Sonora and Chihuahua are capable of running down deer. They watch a herd, pick a specimen, and suddenly appear with yells and shouts while the frightened animals bound away. The hunters chase the chosen deer toward one man stationed in the area, who takes up the chase until the animal drops dead of exhaustion or leaps in panic from a cliff. No weapon is used, only the extraordinary agility of the Indians of this tribe, who are marvelous runners.

11

A Quick Tour of Mexico

The biggest business in Mexico is tourism. Over 800,000 people, chiefly from the United States and Canada, visit annually and in token of their enjoyment leave nearly $8,000,000.

Why do they come in such droves? Ease of entrance and accessibility explain much. You can merely walk across the border to spend a day in a town of northern Mexico. To visit the interior, a United States citizen needs to present only $3, a birth certificate or evidence of citizenship, and proof of smallpox vaccination to receive a tourist card. A trip to Europe is more expensive, more time-consuming in planning and preparation, and requires the red tape of a passport.

A trip to Mexico may be as casual as a ten-day vacation by bus or in the family car to Monterrey, Mexico City, Cuernavaca, and Taxco. Yet such a trip reveals customs, costumes, and a way of life as foreign to ours as those of the Orient.

Once across the Rio Grande, the tourist is in a different world, alien but *simpático* (agreeable, congenial) to those who do not expect life elsewhere to duplicate that in their hometowns. In most of the central plateau the climate is fine at all times of the year; on the coasts and in the lowlands of the interior it is hot. The rainy season, in the summer months, means usually that there is an afternoon rain and then clear weather, so that much of Mexico is delightful all the year. And Mexico has something for every taste—for those who like sports, historical atmosphere, variety of scenery, architecture, photogenic scenes and people, ancient ruins.

A visit to Mexico should not be expected to be an uninterrupted romantic episode, one long, beautiful adventure. In spite of all the beauty and excitement of a strange country, one may be confronted with less amiable aspects, especially outside the favored tourist spots. There *may* be fleas, bedbugs, scorpions, dysentery, tangles with bureaucracy, frustrations, delays, and encounters with squalor and poverty. In case of a highway accident, there is the assumption of the Napoleonic code that you are guilty until proved innocent.

On the other hand, some tourists make their stays needlessly unpleasant by being rude and demanding. They ignore the customs of the country and then are offended when they meet with distrust and dislike. They expect the comforts of home in all situations and make no effort in language or understanding to cross the chasm between cultures.

A traveler who is polite, considerate, and friendly, and makes allowances for odd circumstances is likely to enjoy even the oddities. He brings his welcome with him. In larger cities he may be surprised at the similarities to things at home, at the fine hotels and restaurants, the spacious boulevards and lovely parks, the fascinating shops and stores.

The wise traveler takes care to find out something about

the country in advance so that he comes prepared. Ma-
terially speaking, he brings suitable clothes. For coastal
cities and resorts, he brings beachwear and summer clothing, and girls and women may wear slacks or shorts or
playsuits without offense. It is advisable to carry sweater,
coat, and raincoat for other climates. Although most areas
in the central plateau are warm during the day, even in
the cold months of December, January, and February, almost all cool off remarkably fast at sundown. Certainly
flat sandals or sturdy walking shoes are in order for
the cobblestoned streets or for climbing pyramids and
ruins, and women will want a pair of high-heeled shoes
for dress in the cities. Some clothes the visitor may want
to buy in Mexico—sports shirts, pretty skirts and blouses,
the warm rebozos or quexquemetls, for example. Outside
of resort areas, slacks and shorts for women are frowned
on. In cities, visitors should dress as they do in their cities
at home; in Mexico City suits are desirable for both men
and women, and in the evening a woman may want to dress
as festively as she would in a city at home.

Most travelers spend half their money on restaurants and
purchases, about a fifth for hotels, and another fifth for
transportation. The rest goes for entertainment and mis-
cellaneous expenses. Transportation is cheap. First-class
buses are usually excellent, but if you take an ordinary
bus, don't be surprised if you find some hens cackling in
your face or a baby sitting in your lap. For comfort in
train travel, first-class *special* is recommended, and the
ride is usually more picturesque than rapid. Airplane fares
within the country are low too. Along major highways
are some attractive motels, often with good restaurants.

In smaller cities or off the beaten tourist trails, hotels are often fine old colonial buildings, beautiful and clean, with spacious patios.

The food in all first-class restaurants should be perfectly safe to eat. Little restaurants and cafés serving Mexican food are often very good, but they should be tried on the recommendation of friends or acquaintances in residence, in case of doubt. To be on the safe side, salads and fresh fruits, unless they are peeled, should be avoided. Bottled refreshments are preferable to water if you are in a restaurant of doubtful reputation. Market foods often look and smell tempting, but again it is more discreet to avoid them unless you are with a guide or friend who can advise you on what is safe.

Since the high altitude (usually 5,000 feet and up away from coasts) sometimes affects visitors disagreeably, it is well to take things easy the first few days and neither overeat nor do too much strenuous sightseeing. Siestas are a sensible custom, especially in warm weather.

For most visits to the interior, Mexico City is the focus and the springboard. But the temptation to spend all one's budget for purchases the first few days should be resisted. The bulk of it should be saved for visits to provincial cities, where prices are often lower than in the capital. Seeing shops and markets elsewhere gives the tourist a better idea of values. Haggling can be expected in the markets, but bargaining is rare in good shops and stores. However, one can occasionally take advantage of being the first customer. The clerk or owner may make special concessions because the sale to the first customer is supposed to bring luck for the day.

Border towns are not a fair sampling of Mexican life. They sometimes represent the worst aspects of each country, though there is now a program under way to clean up these towns and make them more attractive.

The Pasco de la Reforma in Mexico City is surely one of the most beautiful avenues in the world. For about four cents you can take a bus trip from the Zócalo at the heart of the city to its outskirts. Along the Reforma, you pass luxury stores, fine hotels and restaurants, circle the *glorietas* (traffic circles) with monuments and flowers and fountains, go through Chapultepec within sight of the castle on its heights. *Insurgentes* and other principal boulevards offer equally beautiful vistas. One-peso cabs course up and down these streets, but for a quarter you can take a taxi to nearby points and for 75 cents, or less, go clear to the outskirts of the city.

Worth a visit are the National Museum of Anthropology, the Palacio Nacional, the Museum of Popular Arts and Crafts, the Palace of Fine Arts (Bellas Artes), and the markets of San Juan de Letrán and the Lagunilla—and plenty of time should be allowed. Sightseeing should include the cathedral and the Shrine of Guadalupe. Chapultepec Park is fine for walking and contains not only the zoo but also historic Chapultepec Castle and the National Historical Museum. Tourists also enjoy watching a charreada on Sunday morning at the Rancho Charro and a game of frontón in the evening.

Visitors find themselves gravitating toward Sanborn's House of Tiles or one of its branches for a reminder of home, and perhaps toward Sears or Woolworth's. They may visit the Biblioteca Benjamin Franklin and the Mexican-North American Cultural Institute, which work for better understanding between the two countries. They may enjoy a visit to the Palacio de Hierro, a fine department store, and they certainly like to stroll along Avenida Juárez or along "Gringo Alley" near the Hotel Géneve.

Popular short trips are to the pyramids of Teotihuacán and to the floating gardens at Xochimilco. And everyone should see the more accessible Pedregal and University City and drive through old San Angel.

The most popular tourist trail leads from Mexico City to Cuernavaca and Taxco and Acapulco. Cuernavaca is the capital of Morelos. Since the days of the Aztecs it has been a favorite weekend resort because of its balmy climate. Cortés's palace with Rivera's murals, the Borda Gardens—a miniature Versailles—and the charming little Sunday market are worth seeing. There is a large colony of foreigners.

Taxco, a mining center, was founded in 1529. It has been made a national colonial monument to preserve its hillside beauty and colonial architecture. The famous Church of Santa Prisca with its twin towers was built by the silver baron José de la Borda. Taxco had become almost a ghost town when William Spratling, a designer of silverwork, settled there in 1931 and began training apprentices. Now the little narrow hilly streets are lined with silver shops, the town is a tourist center, and the apprentices have won themselves reputations. Chief among them are the Castillo brothers, who devised a process of fusing silver with copper and other metals. Spratling's own distinguished work is to be found at his establishment on the highway south of Taxco.

The seaport of Acapulco, once a small fishing village, has in recent decades evolved into a major resort for wealthy Mexicans and North Americans. It is superbly situated on a bay, backed by hills, and boasts splendid beaches and luxurious hotels as well as more modest accommodations. Since 1521 it has been a gateway to South America and later to the Orient. There are boats for fishermen and sailors, launches for trips to coves and inlets, glass-bottomed boats for studying sea life. Fishing, swimming, hunting, harpooning at night, skin diving and water-skiing are among the diversions offered.

Perhaps most different and exciting for the casual visitor is a trip southward which encompasses both cities and archeological sites. Puebla, one of the most Spanish of all Mexican towns, was founded in 1531 by soldiers of Cortés's army. The beautiful cathedral was begun in 1531, and there are dozens of other fine churches. The hidden convent of Santa Monica operated secretly after the abolishment of convents and monasteries in 1857. It is entered through the closet of a humble home and contains many secret passages. The Casa de Alfeñique, once a colonial residence, is now a state museum.

Puebla is known for textiles, serapes, embroidery, and imaginative straw toys. But its greatest fame is as a center of fine pottery and Talavera tiles (inspired by Moorish-Spanish designs), the most beautiful in Mexico. Naturally tile is lavishly used for decoration throughout the city.

According to legend, a Puebla merchant brought here a Chinese princess who was captured by pirates. When she became a Christian, she devised the costume of the china poblana, a bright-colored skirt and embroidered white cotton blouse, popular throughout the country for dancers.

Oaxaca, a quiet colonial city, capital of the State of Oaxaca, on Saturdays explodes into activity with one of the two largest markets in the country. Empty lots and streets fill with burros, buses, high two-wheeled oxcarts, and people, chickens, birds, goats, sheep, pigs, and produce. Campesinos throng past stalls heaped with leather goods; fine knives and machetes with mottos engraved on the blades; huaraches; love potions; herbs for rheumatism, childbirth, and sudden frights. There are whistles and mermaids in black pottery, polychrome clay figures, rebozos, and serapes—some with the Mitla key design.

Soft voices speak dozens of Indian dialects, especially Zapotec. There are tiny girls in creamy white from Yalálag; Mixe women in gray-green tunics; tall, strapping women from the Isthmus of Tehuantepec in ankle-long colorful skirts with lace petticoats and short, sleeveless low-necked blouses, and with heavy gold chains around their necks.

A few miles above the town on a mountain overlooking three valleys is Monte Albán. Several hundred years before Christ this complex of buildings was begun by the Zapotecs, and about 1000 A.D. it was taken over by the Mixtecs. Many of the treasures from the excavated Tomb 7 can be seen in the museum near the main plaza of Oaxaca. Some 30-odd miles from the city is Mitla, City of the Dead, lonely and splendid. It was built a thousand years ago by the Mixtecs in an architectural style suggestive of the Greek and Egyptian buildings, with elaborate mosaics of marvelously set stones.

Mérida, the clean, beautiful colonial capital of Yucatán, was founded in 1542 by the conqueror Francisco de Montejo. The natives dress in immaculate white, frequently in the loose-fitting pleated linen or cotton shirt known as the *guayabera*. The houses are of buff, blue, and pink, with flat roofs. Outlying Indian huts are oval, windowless, thatched with palm leaves like those in ancient Maya murals. Special features of the city are the S-shaped cement love seats (called *confidentes*) in parks and on corners, the windmills, and the *coches* (horse-drawn vehicles).

At Uxmal 50 miles to the west are reconstructed buildings of a ceremonial city of the Maya of the tenth century. Southeast about 75 miles from Mérida is Chichén Itzá. Dating back to the fifth century A.D., it shows the influence of the Plateau Indians on the Maya culture. *El Castillo* (the castle) is the temple of Kukulkán (the Maya Quetzalcoatl), interesting both for its architecture and its astronomical allusions. Four stairways of 91 steps, plus a landing, represent the 365 days of the solar year; the 26 indented surfaces that line the steps on each side represent the 52-year Maya "century." Here too are the Nuns' House, the Temple of the Warriors, the Temple of the Tigers, *El Caracol* (the snail)—a round, observatory-like building—and a huge ball court. Into the nearby sacred *cenote* (well) were flung sacrificial victims. The Mayaland Lodge at Chichén Itzá contains rooms that are replicas of houses in the heart of the forest a thousand years ago.

The Bajío region is the heart of Mexico, its most fertile area, and the cradle of independence. Guanajuato, a beautiful and very Spanish city with narrow, old streets, set amid mountains, grew up around gold and silver mines. The lavishly decorated church of La Valenciana looks down on it near the old quarries. On the other side of the city is the Panteón, a cemetery gruesomely noted for its underground vault of mummies.

More agreeable to visit are the Juárez Theater, an opulent Victorian opera house, and the city market. The market occupies a tremendous vaulted building lined with balconies. The wares range from fantastic clay animals and the tiniest of toy tea sets to gaudy pottery and knitting needles.

Guanajuato is famous for its *Entremeses*. These are little skits, written long ago by the famous Spanish author Cervantes. They are performed on spring nights in the streets of the city. One setting that is used is the stairway leading to a church. Footlights are added to streetlights. Balconies and stairways of neighboring houses are used for other settings. Horses come clattering along the street to take part in the plays. Here too is the University of Guanajuato, whose faculty and students contribute talent for dramas and for the symphony orchestra.

Sixty-odd miles from Guanajuato, by a roundabout route through Dolores Hidalgo, is the lovely hillside city of San Miguel de Allende. Like Taxco, it has been declared a national monument to preserve its colonial atmosphere. Founded about 1542 by Fray Juan de San Miguel, it still has some buildings that date back to the sixteenth century. On Sunday tourists can take the House and Garden Tour for the benefit of the Biblioteca Pública, a rare chance to see something of the life behind the walls of Mexico and the beautiful residences in the city.

The landmark of San Miguel is its old church on the plaza with a weirdly beautiful nineteenth-century pseudo-Gothic façade of pink stone, the design of an untrained local stonemason enchanted by postcards of European Gothic cathedrals. Points of special interest include the public library, the Instituto Allende, the Academia Hispano-Americana, the Galería San Miguel, and the newly restored Cultural Center Ignacio Ramírez, a branch of the Bellas Artes. The Cultural Center houses a small museum of popular arts and crafts and one of anthropology, several galleries of modern and colonial Mexican art, a Siqueiros mural, classrooms for weaving, dancing, music, metalwork, graphics, and even a small theater. Concerts and plays come often to San Miguel, and a large foreign colony has been attracted to the city, drawn by its fine climate, its beauty and history, and its reputation as an art center. The newest project is a resort-riding school, the Escuela Ecuestre S.M.A., at the Rancho Atascadero above the town, featuring instruction by Mexican cavalry officers.

Once called San Miguel el Grande, the city was renamed in honor of its native son, Capt. Ignacio Allende, a hero of the Revolution for Independence. San Miguel is known as a center for the best work in tin, copper, and brass, for fine serapes in the traditional designs and colors of the region as well as in modern themes, and for shops of excellent decor and well-selected products from various regions.

Querétaro, 45 miles away, is capital of the state of that name. The city was the scene not only of a conspiracy that led to revolution, but of the convention that devised the Constitution of 1857 and of the siege, capture, and execution of Emperor Maximilian in 1867.

Its splendid aqueduct dates from the early eighteenth century. From afar Querétaro resembles an Oriental city with its domes and minarets. Within the city are buildings of Spanish and Moorish derivation. It is a busy manufacturing town and a center for the sale of opals.

En route to the capital is San Juan del Río. Here arcades shelter shops whose wares overflow to the edge of the highway. There are serapes from Bernal, basketry from Tequisquiapan, salad bowls, furniture, shoes, guitars, lariats, and products from other regions. A few miles from the main highway to Mexico is the ceremonial city of Tula. Toltecs a thousand years ago built these truncated pyramids with colossal carved figures of stone on top and borders of stone murals of jaguars and eagles on the sides.

One of the most spectacular highways in Mexico leads from the capital to Morelia via Toluca. Toluca, capital of the State of Mexico, is an hour's drive from Mexico City, and on Fridays boasts the most fabulous market in the country. Even on other days it takes hours to inspect it. There are wood carvings, chess sets, furniture; pendants and primitive silver necklaces; woven belts, basketry, rebozos, pottery, and embroidery. The Museum of Popular Arts and Crafts is one of the finest in the country.

Morelia, once called Valladolid, was renamed for its native son, Father Morelos, another hero of Independence. Here too was born Iturbide, later Emperor of Mexico.

Morelia is the capital of Michoacán and has many handsome colonial houses, palaces, plazas, and churches. Its beautiful cathedral dates back to 1640-1744. It has industrial schools, the Colegio San Nicolas, a fine state library, a state museum, and a branch of the Mexican-North American Cultural Institute. The Casa Cerda is an excellent shop run by two talented sisters who create beautiful lacquerware, embroidery, and rebozos. Outside the city on a mountainside is the Villa Montaña, a hotel with a superb cuisine.

The Tarascans who inhabited the Michoacán region were a cultured, peaceful, and industrious people with a language different from all the others of Mexico. Fiercely independent, they resisted even the Spaniards until the kindly Bishop Vasco de Quiroga came to work for their welfare and won their devotion.

The village of Tzintzuntzan on Lake Pátzcuaro was once the capital of the populous Tarascan empire. The ancestors of these villagers were skilled potters. The sculptress Helen O'Gorman has stimulated a rebirth of good glazed ware, using native motifs of village life on a cream or chocolate-brown base. The UNESCO training center for rural teachers on Lake Pátzcuaro has helped local potters to devise better formulas for clay, glazes, and firing techniques.

Farther along Lake Pátzcuaro is the charming city of Pátzcuaro. It has a spectacular Friday market attended by women in heavy wide skirts of red or black wool, rebozos of black cotton with stripes, and crosses of fine silver filigree or primitive hammered solid silver around their necks. The fishermen from the island of Janitzio paddle across the lake with their butterfly nets, and the total effect is very colorful. Unfortunately, the weather tends to be less inviting than in some other areas of Mexico, though still pleasant by most United States standards. Certain villages in the area specialize in different crafts. There is copperware from Santa Clara del Cobre, lacquerware from Uruapan, embroidery from the lake towns, Tarascan jewelry, pottery from Patumba—all can be found in the market.

The Pátzcuaro Museum of Popular Arts and Archeology, once the school of Quiroga, contains exhibits of old pottery, lacquerwork, and colonial retablos. The public library contains a mural by Juan O'Gorman. Another Casa Cerda, run by the aunt of the Cerda sisters of Morelia, is virtually a museum of traditional arts.

Janitzio is famous for its celebration of the Day of the Dead. Although a nightlong vigil is held in cemeteries all over Mexico on November 1-2, the ceremony here seems more picturesque. The islanders come with baskets of food, candles, and bouquets of marigolds and spread their offerings on the graves of those they have come to visit.

Northwest of the lake towns is Guadalajara, second-largest city in Mexico and capital of Jalisco. One of the pleasures of visiting this colonial city is sightseeing from a *calandria*, a little horse-drawn vehicle which moves at an amiable pace through the streets and parks. Among the industries of the city are glassware, shoes, textiles, and flour. More romantically it is known as the home of the mariachis and the national dance, the jarabe tapatío. Fine Orozco murals are here at the Governor's Palace and *El Hospicio de Niños* (the orphanage) and also the Orozco Museum, which was the artist's home. The University of Guadalajara, established in 1792, attracts both Mexican and American students.

In Guadalajara the mariachis are as necessary for parties as ice cream is for a birthday party in the United States. They sing such favorites as *"Si Estás Dormida"* (If You Are Asleep), *"Las Mañanitas,"* and ranch songs.

Tarascan, Huichol, and Cora Indians live in the area, and occasionally visit the city. The Huichol Indians wear flat-crowned hats adorned with flowers and feathers and carry handsomely woven wool and cotton pouches dangling from their belts.

A high point of the year is the welcome home of the dark-skinned Virgin of Zapopan. She is so popular that for four months she journeys around the region and spends a few days in each church. When she returns on October 4 to her own sanctuary near the city, hundreds of thousands join in a procession to honor her with songs and dances.

Near Guadalajara are other towns of interest. Tlaquepaque and Tonalá are pottery centers. Lake Chapala, the largest in Mexico, has the Bohemian art colony of Ajijíc and the more conservative resort village of Chapala, much patronized by retired foreign military personnel. On the seacoast, 45 minutes by plane from Guadalajara, is the increasingly popular small resort of Puerto Vallarta.

The third-largest city of the Republic is Monterrey, capital of Nuevo León and a stopover on the highway to Mexico City. It is foremost a business town, efficient, Americanized, full of traffic, excellent hotels, and stores and factories. It is an industrial center, with famous breweries, and produces glass, steel, cement, and furniture also.

The city takes great pride in its State University of Nuevo León and the fine new *Instituto Tecnológico*. The latter is staffed by very good and reasonably well-paid professors, has a splendid library, modern buildings, and is attended by Americans as well as Mexicans. Other institutions include the Alvaro Obregón Vocational School, a good hospital, and the beautiful contemporary Church of the Virgin of the Immaculate Conception.

Most important of the seaports, and the first Spanish settlement, is Veracruz. It is cosmopolitan, gay and picturesque, tropical in feeling, and it smacks of Afro-Cuban culture. Night life in Veracruz, unlike that of many Mexican cities, is lively. At carnival time its citizens go quite mad with costumes, parades, clowns, and balls.

This has been a mere sampling of some of the cities most favored by tourists. Each corner of the country holds its own surprises and delights in scenery and crafts and architecture. Each has a different personality.

Every visitor has his favorite spots, and no one who loves Mexico can be totally satisfied with another's account of it. A trip south of the border is the best way to learn the charms of Mexico.

12

What If . . . and What Next?

What is the attitude of Mexicans toward the United States of America? It is a shifting pattern, depending on circumstances and world events, tentative—admiring and jealous, friendly and hostile by turns, but always fiercely independent and not completely trusting.

Perhaps it can best be understood by recasting history in a "let's suppose" vein.

Let us imagine that the colonies of North America had not succeeded in their revolution but had remained under British rule until 1821. Let us suppose that missionaries, traders, and explorers had extended British dominion over most of North America.

Pretend now that Canada had become independent in the late eighteenth century. It had consolidated its territory, supplemented its agriculture with industry, and become a powerful neighbor. Meantime the colonies were still ruled by deputies of the Crown, were still exporting all raw material to the mother country, and were fettered by restrictions on trade, commerce, and manufacturing.

What *might* have happened?

Picture Canada, cramped into the eastern part of its domain, seeking room for its growing population. It becomes more aggressive, gradually expands west and south, and its citizens eventually populate much of Wisconsin,

Minnesota, North and South Dakota. At last in 1821 the American colonies win independence. While they are still weak from war, dissension, and disorganization, severed from the protection of Britain, the clashes begin between the Americans and the Candian interlopers.

In this presumed history, in the 1830's a Canadian army invades the Northwest and engineers the separation of the region as the Republic of the Northwest. In 1845 Canada admits the Republic as a province and becomes even more powerful. There soon follows a war—with reckless disregard of Canada's own proclamation that it would protect weaker countries of the hemisphere from aggression by other powers. An invading army penetrates to the capital at Philadelphia, which is also the largest city of the young nation. The United States, demoralized and at odds, capitulates. It signs a treaty dictated by the conqueror and cedes most of the land west of the Mississippi with the token compensation of a few million dollars. The Americans make national heroes of the young cadets at West Point who courageously tried to defend that bulwark against much larger forces.

From that point on, the United States struggles to regain its equilibrium, but it is torn by internal conflict and by intervention of a European power that places a puppet emperor on the throne of the United States. When the foreigner is ousted, a dictator comes to power who rules for thirty-some years. He brings railroads, foreigners, and foreign investments which give the nation status in the world and further enrich the wealthy class of the country, but at the cost of keeping most of the people ill fed, ill clothed, ill housed, and with no opportunity to better themselves.

In 1910 begins a revolution led by a gentleman farmer, bandit generals, and rebellious peasants. The gentleman farmer is made President, to the distress of foreign interests who have favored the dictator. The President is betrayed by a former supporter and deposed. The Canadian Ambassador intervenes without leave from his government—and the President is shortly afterwards shot "while trying to escape."

Although this Ambassador is recalled, relations between the two countries continue to be strained. Canadian sailors carousing in the port of New York are arrested by American authorities. In revenge the Canadians land marines, and a skirmish follows. An American farmer with some followers crosses the border to the north and kills thirty Canadians in nearby towns, and a Canadian punitive expedition of 12,000 men once more invades the United States to capture the leader. It fails and the farmer becomes a hero of folklore and ballads.

In 1917 a new constitution is framed. For a few years various strong men jockey for power and become wealthy while some of the new principles in the Constitution are applied, in education and in land distribution. For the next few years there are rebellions and assassinations. Eventually the political situation steadies, following the expropriation of foreign holdings and the nationalization of coal and oil industries. Though still very poor, the country turns gradually to industry, improves its literacy, sanitation, and agricultural methods, and begins to manufacture items long available only by importation. A period of relative prosperity and stability begins, and a more cooperative condition prevails between the two neighbors.

Nevertheless, United States citizens do not easily forget

Canadian intervention in their domestic affairs, nor the invasions. The saying among them is that Canada wants democracy for itself but not for others.

All of the foregoing *might* have happened to the United States if history had followed a slightly different course. It *did* happen in the relationship between Mexico and the United States, with Mexico on the short end of the stick. This "let's suppose" may provide some idea of why Mexicans have mixed feelings toward the United States as a nation instead of accepting our own view of our country as the Don Quixote of democracy.

Some Americans in public life have helped to allay the natural distrust of the Mexicans. Ambassador Dwight Morrow significantly changed tradition by his friendliness toward the Mexican people and their government in contrast to his predecessors, who linked themselves only with the narrow interests of the rich American colony. When President Truman visited Mexico in 1947, he won Mexican hearts by his simple offering of flowers at the monument to the Niños Héroes—the boys who had given their lives in trying to defend Chapultepec against the American invaders—in token of the United States's recognition of the injustice of that war.

The tremendous popularity of President and Mrs. Kennedy in their 1962 visit to Mexico has also greatly influenced the development of a new climate of accord between the United States and Mexico. President Kennedy came in the hope of advancing the cause of the Alliance for Progress in Latin America and promoting hemispheric unity and friendship between his people and Mexico. His recognition that "the fundamental goal of the Mexican

Revolution is the same as that of the Alliance for Progress; social justice and economic progress within a framework of political and individual freedom" was acknowledged by President López Mateos in his speech to the nation in September, 1962.

There are prickly matters to be dealt with. Among them are a solution to the problem of the contaminating salts in the Colorado River that damage Mexican crops, adjustment of the land in dispute between the two countries since the Rio Grande altered its course in 1864, and a fair handling of the problem of the braceros.

During World War II when manpower in the United States was sharply reduced because of the draft, 50,000 braceros were hired as migrant farm workers, to be paid at regular United States wages. There was a stampede to apply, and thousands of Mexicans were smuggled illegally across the border besides. Many were fleeced by unscrupulous Mexicans and Americans—and some were murdered. Workers who had entered illegally were often abused, underpaid, or not paid at all, but they did not dare make complaints. Many, of their own accord, had swum across the Rio Grande to work –hence the term "wetback."

On the Mexican side there was resentment of this sometimes brutal treatment. On the American side native workers felt that imported labor, often underpaid, was a threat to their livelihood. So what might have been a useful experiment in international living and education became a potential danger. A great number of Mexicans who had suffered abuse and injustice from unscrupulous employers came back with natural prejudices. But the lure of higher wages is keen, and many thousands still risk danger and ill treatment for the chance to bring back money. Fortunately, other thousands return to Mexico with more money than they have ever had, enthusiasm for American methods of farming and raising livestock, and valuable experience with American customs, sanitation, and language.

Generally speaking, these workers, who pass stringent tests to qualify as braceros, are good representatives of their country. Their courtesy, appreciation of good treatment and food, and their willingness to work hard create an excellent impression. Unfortunately, in some areas, they encounter such prejudice that the Mexican government blacklists certain counties in the United States. The need to work out a satisfactory solution is acute. Stricter supervision on both sides of the border would help.

Mexico fears the abandonment of its own farmland, which is direly needed, and also fears that too many braceros will want to remain abroad. But most of these Mexicans, though they may admire our country and crave its products and opportunities, deeply love their own land and want to return to it with a stake to improve their condition at home.

In the field of foreign affairs, unrest in Mexico and suspicion of United States foreign policy have been created by the disastrous Bay of Pigs invasion attempt to overthrow the Castro regime in Cuba and by later efforts to pressure Mexico into following United States policy in dealing with Cuba. There have been some riots and demonstrations against the United States.

However, certain United States news magazines and newspapers carry exaggerated accounts of Mexican opinion and activities without presenting the framework in which these exist. Each such adverse report reputedly costs Mexico 10,000 tourists who decide to go elsewhere.

Many factors, which are not always taken into account, enter the picture. Often such anti-American demonstrations are caused more by jealousy of the success of a foreign enterprise or by personal reasons than by any profound political conviction. In most parts of Mexico a thriving business is apt to be headed by a foreigner, though a new Mexican generation is growing up with a dynamic sense of business and a responsible attitude toward schedules, deadlines, and efficiency that are necessary for the functioning of large-scale business. Some demonstrations are initiated and even subsidized by foreign agents. It should be noted that there are frequent counterdemonstrations too, which show sympathy for the United States.

The role of ex-President Lázaro Cárdenas should not be minimized. He is beloved by the people for his great contributions to their welfare during his administration, and he has emerged from private life with a distinctly Communist-oriented pattern of activity. Because of his great prestige, he still exerts immense influence, especially among the campesinos, the students, and the people of his home state of Michoacán. After an inflammatory speech to some 6,000 students in the main plaza of the capital, he triggered a pro-Castro and anti-American riot in Morelia. There, demonstrators besieged the Mexican-North American Cultural Institute, forced some North American residents to flee by way of rooftops and fire escapes, beat up one, and burned the library and the contents of the building. The presence of Russian residents in Morelia may be more than coincidence. However, the Institute has since been restocked and reopened and is functioning again, thanks partly to the help of Mexican sympathizers with the United States. The feeling in the region of Michoacán is not representative of the atmosphere prevalent in most other areas of Mexico.

The present regime under President Adolfo López Mateos is clearly eager to preserve the friendship of the United States. One of the President's speeches states forthrightly: "My government stands ready to repress all excesses by demagogical groups or individuals, from the right or the left." Some measures have been taken to cope with the left. The artist Siqueiros and other leftist leaders have been jailed. When a Latin American Conference was promoted by the Cuban Embassy with Russian support, the only hall available was one on the outskirts of Mexico City. Only 2,000 or so attended in a city of nearly 5,000,000 people. Only about 250 of some 1,500 expected delegates showed up. On the second day only two-thirds of the hall was filled, and the Mexican press and radio gave the conference no publicity.

It should be pointed out that although all the ex-presidents of Mexico have some official post in this administration, Cárdenas was assigned a responsible one but one not connected with policy-making. He was made Chairman of the Hydroelectric Commission. The most prominent post, that of president of the National Council of Tourism, went to ex-president Miguel Alemán, a firm supporter of capitalism and friendship with the United States.

Is Mexico likely to turn Communist? It is a country with a history of violence and cataclysmic changes, a people so volatile that it would be a reckless prophet who would try to pin it down to rigid analysis or forecasting.

The diligence, patience, and willingness of Russian strate-
gists must not be underestimated. When an American Ambassador visited a library founded by foreigners and turned
into a cooperative project for native and foreign residents
alike, he praised the project enthusiastically and promised
to inform the President about so worthwhile an achievement. That was gratifying to the founders. When the Russian Ambassador visited, he did not speak of notifying
Nikita Khrushchev—but he did send books for the children in Spanish that might in time influence some young
readers.

In a country with vast numbers of the underprivileged,
there are always potential Communists ripe for the pluck-
ing, especially idealistic young students with more opti-
mism than political sagacity. There is still an immense gulf
between the millionaires of the country and the campesinos
who earn less than $300 a year. But growing economic
prosperity is gradually bridging that gulf, and the expanding middle class is fervently capitalistic. The Mexican
temperament (if you can speak of *one* in a country whose
inhabitants vary so remarkably) is generally so individual-
istic and in some respects so changeable—and full of humor
—that it would not be easy to encase it in a straitjacket of
Marxism. The total membership of the Communist party
is estimated at less than 10,000 in the whole country.
And the "Colossus of the North" is still an image to envy
and conjure with, far more potent and vivid to the Mexican
than distant Russia.

The promise seems to be for increased stability in government and for gradual strengthening of the institutions
favoring democracy. The continuity of presidential re-
gimes for several decades has proceeded without marked

violence or armed revolts, in contrast to the former frequency of rebellion and assassination.

"Free enterprise, nationalism, and administrative improvement are in vogue in Mexico today," says William P. Tucker in *The Mexican Government Today*. ". . . If the trend toward honesty and integrity in government continues, Mexico can go a long way . . . toward becoming an important modern country."

A recent survey by *Visión*, a leading news magazine of Latin America, through interviews with diplomats, newsmen, industrialists, and ranchers, asked four questions:

What is the current state of Inter-American relationships?

What brought them to this point?

What can the United States do about it?

What can Latin America do about it?

Only four out of fifty respondents thought the relationship cordial. Eight believed there has been recent improvement, but most agreed that relations have seldom been worse.

Why? Chiefly because of United States neglect and ignorance, they believe. Latin Americans feel that we ignore them until a crisis comes, that if we devoted as much attention and generosity to them as we do to some other countries, the effect would be much happier. An editor added: "The U.S. must persist in aiding democracy, in fighting dictatorships, and in helping to raise living standards. . . . In all this, it must choose the executors of its policies with more care."

If we protest that it is unfair to charge us with such responsibilities, we must answer ourselves that we have led the world to expect it, that we have assumed them elsewhere, and why not for our immediate neighbors? Mexico has an obligation on its part to promote good relations, and we have ours.

It would help if all United States citizens resident in Mexico or visiting, both private and official, would realize that they bear a responsibility to cement favorable relations by using common sense, good will, courtesy, and sensitivity to the needs and feelings of the Mexican hosts. It would help if they could work formally or informally with the Mexicans in establishing libraries, hospitals, clinics, and in teaching techniques of farming, sanitation, and diet, as many have already done.

The Biblioteca Benjamin Franklin, an invaluable institution in Mexico City, with branches in Guadalajara and Monterrey, has proved itself a creator of friendly relations, and more such projects should be encouraged. It brings art exhibits to both Mexicans and foreigners, sends for books unobtainable in Mexico on interlibrary loans, provides reading, study, and microfilm facilities, and sponsors other cultural activities with courtesy, warmth, and efficiency. The Mexican-North American Cultural Institute has a similar fine record of cooperation.

Among the most effective projects in international relations has been the extremely successful tour of the Harvard-Radcliffe Orchestra in 1962. The seventy students involved raised most of the $52,500 necessary for the trip, made the plans, which included concerts at low cost or free or for the benefit of local charities, concerts with Mexican soloists and/or conductors, demonstration lectures for schools and colleges by small chamber groups, and finding accommodations in both Mexican and foreign homes for the students. Musically and individually, the group impressed Mexicans most favorably and demonstrated convincingly the great interest our young people have in Mexico. This was followed in 1963 by a tour made by the Smith-Wesleyan choir.

It would help if our United States tourists went to Mexico with a better understanding of the country and preferably with some knowledge of the Spanish language, with more awareness of our own history and with more respect for the cultural assets of the host country. But understanding of a foreign country and its people is harder to bring back than silver jewelry and basketware.

It would help if the United States government consistently selected the best of diplomatic personnel to represent us abroad. This means people who speak the language, know the history, have some understanding of the country, as well as a keen sense of the urgency of building good relations with the United States. In Mexico, of all countries, it is vital to delegate people who are simpático, with warmth and concern for other humans.

It would help if we could recognize that although the people of Latin America share our aspirations for freedom and well-being, their way of attaining them may differ. We must realize that other countries can achieve some of our goals by methods more appropriate to their society and not insist on a duplication of ours.

The counsel of ex-President Alemán through the channel of the important Tourist Department has done much to iron out the confusions and thorny problems that once plagued American residents and tourists and to make them feel like welcome guests. New regulations permit short visits to Mexico for 50 cents, allow retired foreigners to bring household goods and their own cars to Mexico, and coordinate permits for cars with the six-month tourist cards. Activities among various government departments are arranged to facilitate instead of hinder matters for foreigners. On major highways service jeeps are manned by English-speaking drivers and mechanics trained in first aid as well as in dealing with breakdowns of cars. In effect, visitors find life much easier than was possible under former laws. Mexico too is trying to do its part in promoting good relations.

A long-time North American resident of Mexico said once that a foreigner passes through three stages of reactions to Mexico and its people. In the first, he is infatuated with the alternately stark and lavish beauty of the land and by the romantic simplicity of its people. In the second phase, he turns sour and discovers the aridity and harshness of life caused by geographic factors and a long history of oppression, and becomes infuriated, frustrated, and disillusioned by inefficiency and unnecessary delays and complications. In the third he achieves a more realistic perspective. He enjoys again the beauty and simplicity while he remains aware of the injustice of expecting a people so different in their traditions and outlook to conform to his particular standards.

Neither Mexican culture nor ours can be refashioned in the image of the other, but we can each gain something from the other.

Mexican society typically lacks cohesion, solidarity, and collective enterprise. Individuality is the rule, and the Mexican speaks for himself. He is not a spokesman for a group. His orientation is poetic and romantic and emotional. He follows faith, heart, and sentiment, whereas we stress reason, common sense, and scientific and business standards. The Mexican places high value on art, literature, personal dignity, heroism, religious experience, and a rich interior life. He is short on organization and efficiency, which are our forte. He feels that the North American's tendency to speak constantly of business matters and commonplaces is indicative of superficiality.

He has feelings of inferiority. Proximity to the power of the United States; the small stature characteristic of a generally undernourished people; the insistence for centuries by the Spaniards that the native Indian culture was inferior—all these blend to undermine the confidence of the average Mexican, though there are many exceptions to these generalities. Hence the stress on the concept of the *machismo*, the real he-man. Hence also the riotous and reckless driving so typical of the traffic in the capital and many other sections of the country. It is a sort of dramatization of resentment, a dream of power and glory realized.

So there is a constant swing between opposites: timidity and bravado; humor and solemnity; violence and gentleness; reserve which on acceptance of an outsider turns into wholehearted friendliness and confidence. The average Mexican has so little in the way of possessions that size and quantity have little meaning for him. Instead he values quality, is fond of diminutive objects and animals, carves intricate scenes in a nutshell. He constantly uses the suffix -*ito*, which connotes smallness and tenderness, in such words as *monito* (little monkey), *mamacita* (little mother), *gatito* (kitty), *hermanito* (little brother), or even in abstract words like *momentito* (just a second), *ahorita* (right away), *tantito* (a tiny bit). Furthermore, when he speaks of a favorite saint, he is likely to use this suffix. San Miguel, for example, becomes San Miguelito.

The Mexican is a great mimic and imitator, quick to learn new skills. He has become a good mechanic and operator of cars and tractors (if he were not an expert driver, he could not survive the maelstrom of Mexican traffic). His laziness is a myth. Given proper diet and working conditions, he puts his heart and soul into his work and takes a personal pride in it. Then he relaxes completely. He can improvise brilliantly, not only in forming a constitution and a new economy but in repairing a watch, tractor, or automobile.

The average United States citizen lives on a scale that can be equaled only by a Mexican of wealth. He takes for granted cars, bathrooms, central heating, tools, stoves, dishwashers, refrigerators. But he is at the mercy of any breakdown in the economy or in communications. He needs a specialist for any disruption of plumbing or electricity. He has little time for gardening, carpentry, or painting, especially if he plays golf or tennis or bowls. The current trend toward do-it-yourself and emphasis on more creative hobbies away from business, commuting, and civic meetings suggests a recognition of the need for participation that is so characteristic of the Mexican culture. The North American is oriented toward materialistic possessions and judgments ("I earn more than my neighbor and therefore must be more successful"). These are not absent from the Mexican culture, but they are much less stressed.

On the other hand, much of Mexican life is on a bare subsistence level. Even so, it is more independent of the fluctuations of its economy and more self-sufficient. There is almost no unemployment.

The Mexican of the lower classes can build and maintain his own home, according to his needs. He grows his food or barters it at the market. He makes the very material for his house of adobe brick and thatched maguey. In his spare time he makes pottery for the kitchen or clay toys or weaves a serape. There is no dependence on the drugstore, supermarket, or hardware store, without which the North American can scarcely exist.

Yet the middle-class and upper-class Mexicans live in a manner very like ours. They are fully as dependent as we are on tradesmen, and the national picture is shifting in this direction.

The Mexican needs a higher average level of living, clothing, diet, housing, relief from long hours of toil, and better medical care and health. We need his homely accomplishments, the habit of participation rather than spectatorship, the creative satisfactions, and self-sufficiency.

Tzentzenhuaro is a village near Pátzcuaro, a row of adobe houses with red-tiled roofs, a church and school side by side, and hens wandering down its single unpaved street. How is it different from any village of the underprivileged areas?

You reach the village over a new dirt road. You see pipes for a new water supply by the roadside. An open-air theater stands on the square. There is an asphalt basketball court, built by the villagers. Children are studying in a new school. New seeds are being planted, new trees are growing in the orchards. Men meet once a week to talk and read newspapers and hear what is going on in the world. The women cook over high stoves instead of bending over stones placed on the ground where babies and animals are crawling and running around. The villagers are excited about their discovery of the alphabet and reading.

It is a village whose people are alive, not merely subsisting.

In 1951 UNESCO opened its first class of 52 students from Latin America at the Regional Center for Fundamental Education in Latin America—known in Spanish as CREFAL—near Pátzcuaro. Nurses, agricultural engineers, teachers, and social workers come to learn how to educate their own people in the fundamentals of good living. The staff is international and its work is supported by UN agencies (Food and Agriculture Organization, International Labor Organization, and the World Health Organization), as well as by UNESCO, the Organization of American States, UN technical assistance, and the Mexican government.

When the team of five from UNESCO first visited the village of Tzentzenhuaro, the people were polite but reserved. The visitors explained that the village needed a pure water supply, latrines, a campaign against lice, a way of improving the farmers' yield, and the opportunity of learning to read and write. The villagers listened courteously and then ignored them. The newcomers visited homes and fields, played (and lost) a game of basketball with the youngsters on a dirt court.

As an opening wedge in the process of becoming a part of village life, the newcomers used what they discovered were the villagers' two ambitions—to rebuild the school and to make a good basketball court. An improvement committee was formed. It saw the need for a road to allow the hauling in of sand and asphalt for the court, so each man was drafted to work two days a week on the road. The road was built, and then the school and the basketball court. An old warehouse was whitewashed and dressed up as a social center. By then the visitors were accepted as friends, advisers, and participants, and work went ahead with other projects.

This story has been repeated with variations in other villages. In Cucuchucho, for example, it took an epidemic of typhoid and ten deaths to start the new program. The recreation specialist, who adds the zest of games and fun to keep young and old busy and entertained, is indispensable in selling the new ideas. Canoe races, competitions in marbles, Chinese checkers, jumping rope, and basketball, duck hunting with harpoons—all are part of the repertoire. Dances, music, acting, and dressing up in local costume for fiestas and traditional dances are encouraged.

Literacy fairs with theater and puppet stages and exhibits are used to stimulate the people. A photographic exhibit shows the advantages of a man who can read over his illiterate neighbor. A film strip tells the story of an illiterate man who gave his sick child the wrong medicine. The audience waits tensely for the outcome and demands a second showing. Evening classes are started for adults in reading and other subjects, and the center's librarian issues books. Unable to wait, some of the villagers sit down in the middle of the road to hear a reader tell them on the spot what is in the book. Even a hand printing press is set up.

This project spreads its influence in ever-widening circles throughout Latin America, bringing fundamental education to remote villages in a way that they can understand, with immediate benefits.

It is well to remember that geographically and culturally Mexico is the bridge between the United States and Central and South America. It is our primary contact and a leader among our southern neighbors. If we succeed in cementing good relations with Mexico, it is the signpost of success with the whole hemisphere.

But political considerations are logical and cold. What the Mexican holds dear are warmth and understanding, not logic and calculation. The password is *amistad*, a friendship from which both nations can learn.

Bibliography

Augur, Helen. *Zapotec.* Garden City, N.Y.: Doubleday & Co., 1954.

Banco Nacional de Comercio Exterior, S.A. (author and publisher). *Mexico, 1960.* Mexico, D.F.: 1960.

Blasio, José Luis. *Maximilian Emperor of Mexico, Memoirs of His Private Secretary.* Translated and edited by Robert Hammond Murray. New Haven, Conn.: Yale University Press, 1934.

Brenner, Anita. *Idols Behind Altars.* New York: Payson and Clarke, 1929.

Bush Romero, Pablo. *Mexico and Africa.* México: Gráfica Panamérica.

Calderón de la Barca, Frances. *Life in Mexico.* Garden City, N.Y.: Doubleday & Co., 1842.

Cárdenas, Edouardo. *Anuario Mundial, 1961.* New York: Editor's Press Service, 1960.

Caruso, John Anthony. *The Liberators of Mexico.* New York: Pageant Press, 1954.

Chase, Stuart. *Mexico, a Study of Two Americas.* New York: The Macmillan Co., 1931.

Cintrón, Lala Verrill. *Goddess of the Bullring: The Story of Conchita Cintron.* Indianapolis and New York: Bobbs-Merrill Co., 1960.

Cortés, Hernando. *Five Letters, 1519-1526.* Translated by

J. Bayard Morris. London: George Routledge & Sons, 1928.

Corti, Egon Caesar Count. *Maximilian and Charlotte of Mexico*. Translated from the German by Catherine Alison Phillips. Vol. 2. New York: Alfred A. Knopf, 1929.

Cotner, T. E., and Castenada, Carlos E. (eds.). *Essays in Mexican History*. Austin: University of Texas Press, 1958.

Crow, John Armstrong. *The Epic of Latin America*. Garden City, N.Y.: Doubleday & Co., 1946.

———. *Mexico Today*. New York: Harper & Bros., 1957.

Díaz del Castillo, Bernal. *The Bernal Díaz Chronicles*. Translated and edited by Albert Idell. Garden City, N.Y.: Doubleday & Co., 1956.

Evergreen Review. "The Eye of Mexico." Vol. 2, No. 7 (Winter, 1959).

Fergusson, Erna. *Mexico Revisited*. New York: Alfred A. Knopf, 1955.

Flandrau, Charles. *Viva México!* New York: Harper & Bros., 1908.

Ford, Norman. *Mexico: Where Everything Costs Less*. Green Lawn, N.Y.: Harian Publications, 1962.

Gillmor, Frances. *Flute of the Smoking Mirror*. Albuquerque, N. Mex.: University of New Mexico Press, 1949.

Gomez de Orozco, Federico. *Doña Marina, La Dama de la Conquista*. (Vidas Mexicanas.) Mexico: Ediciones Zochitl, 1942.

Hagen, Victor W. Von. *World of the Maya*. New York: New American Library of World Literature, 1960.

Hanke, Lewis U. *Bartolomé de las Casas: Historian*. Gainesville, Fla.: University of Florida Press, 1952.

James, Daniel. *How to Invest and Live in Mexico*. San Carlos, Calif.: Nourse Publishing Co., 1960.

Langer, William (ed.). *An Encyclopedia of World History*. Boston: Houghton Mifflin, 1952.

Lewis, Oscar. *The Children of Sánchez*. New York: Random House, 1962.

———. *Five Families, Mexican Case Studies in the Culture of Poverty*. New York: Basic Books, 1959.

Linati, Claudio. *Trajes Civiles, Militares, y Religiosos de México*. Mexico, D.F.: Universidad Nacional Autónoma de México, 1956.

Long, Haniel. *Malinche* (Doña Marina). Santa Fe, N. Mex.: Rydal Press, 1939.

Mathews, Wendell. *Essence Versus Appearance: An Interview with Tamayo*. Thesis for MFA degree, Instituto Allende, San Miguel de Allende, Gto., Mexico, 1961.

Myers, I. E. *Mexico's Modern Architecture*. New York: Architectural Book Publishing Co., 1952.

National Geographic Society. *Indians of the Americas*. Washington, D.C.: Natl. Geographic Society, 1955.

Norman, James. *In Mexico: Where to Look and How to Buy Popular Arts and Crafts*. New York: William Morrow and Co., 1959.

Prescott, William H. *Conquest of Mexico and the Conquest of Peru*. New York: Modern Library.

Redfield, Robert. *Tepoztlan, A Mexican Village*. Chicago, Ill.: University of Chicago Press, 1930.

Ross, Patricia Fent. *Made in Mexico*. New York: Alfred A. Knopf, 1952.

Sanderson, Ivan T. *Living Mammals of the World*. New York: Doubleday & Co., 1955.

Schlarman, Joseph H. *Mexico, A Land of Volcanoes, from Cortés to Alemán.* Milwaukee, Wis.: Bruce Publishing Co., 1950.

Scott, Robert E. *Mexican Government in Transition.* Urbana, Ill.: University of Illinois Press, 1959.

Simpson, Lesley Byrd. *Many Mexicos.* Berkeley and Los Angeles, Calif.: University of California Press, 1959.

Smart, Charles Allen. *At Home in Mexico.* New York: Doubleday & Co., 1957.

Tannenbaum, Frank. *Mexico, the Struggle for Peace and Bread.* New York: Alfred A. Knopf, 1950.

Terry, T. Philip. *Guide to Mexico.* Chestnut Hill, Mass.: R. C. Terry, 1947.

Toor, Frances. *A Treasury of Mexican Folkways.* New York: Crown Publishers, 1947.

Torres-Ríoseco, Arturo. *The Epic of Latin American Literature.* Berkeley and Los Angeles: University of California Press, 1942.

Tucker, William P. *Mexican Government Today.* Minneapolis, Minn.: University of Minnesota Press, 1957.

Vaillant, George Clapp. *The Aztecs of Mexico.* Baltimore, Md.: Penguin Books, 1944.

Verissimo, Erico. *Mexico.* Translated from the Portuguese by Linton Barrett. New York: Orion Press, 1960.

Weyer, Edward M. *Primitive Peoples Today.* New York: Doubleday & Co., 1959.

Index

217